Poems,
Prayers
&
Spiritual Verse

To all who have bought this book, thank you.

All I ask is when you read the poems, you open your eyes, your heart and your mind.

God Bless and Believe

Bill Hulme

Table of contents

BEGINNING

Creation

1st Day of God's creation
The heavens and earth took form.
The earths' void was full of darkness
So God made light the earth to warm.
Gods' spirit hovered over waters,
Observing all around,
He'd given light to split the darkness,
And through its' denseness it was wound.

2nd day the waters parted,
Some on high and some below.
The upper waters were called heaven,
Because God had named them so.
An expanse God had created,
To continue as it should,
Separating all the waters,
God looked and it was good.

The 3rd day God gathered water,
In one place then formed the earth,
Which he now covered with vegetation,
As individual seeds gave birth
Yielding fruits according to each kind,
They grew with plants and trees,
For God had placed the dry land,
A different position from the seas.

The 4th day God made the planets,
As lights hanging in the sky,
Being signs for days and seasons,
And for years which will pass by.
Two great lights he then created,
Positioning them at his chosen height,
The sun ruled over daytime,
The moon ruled over night.

The 5th day God filled the waters,
With swarms of living things,
And birds flew across the heavens,
Propelled by the power of their wings.
God told all animals to be fruitful,
Populating all the earth.
Since then animals have procreated,
As each type continues to give birth.

The 6th day brought all the creatures,
Each as according to their kind.
Then God made man in his own image,
Complete in body and in mind.
He said "Let man have dominion,
Over all beasts that roam the earth.
With power to control and rule them,
They are superior in their birth".

The 7th day God, he rested,
His creation was complete.
And Christ who was there with him,
Was given a footstool for his feet.
God saw all he'd made was perfect,
God saw all he'd made was good.
He'd provided for His chosen,
Just like a Father should.

And there began the greatest story,
In the history of man.
Each piece part of Gods jigsaw,
Each piece part of Gods plan.
And for you if you are searching,
Will find it all inside his book,
A record has been kept for us,
All you need to do is look.

First Sin

Adam lived inside the garden
Given lordship over all
The beasts that roamed across the earth,
And birds in the trees so tall.
His life was mainly happy,
Until loneliness appeared,
I need someone who's like me
Is what the father heard.

A deep sleep Adam entered,
And God a rib removed,
And formed Adam's companion
God's care for Adam now He'd proved.
Both labouring in the garden
Tending to all the plants within
They knew all the Lord had told them
But they knew not how to sin.

From the first day in the garden
God had put them both in charge.
Telling both they could have all things
Whether they are small or large.
There was only one condition
And that concerned the tree of life
If of its fruit they tasted,
They would experience death and strife.

In bliss they both existed
Each fulfilled in every need,
Till one day in the garden
Eve encountered Satan's seed.
In the form of a lowly serpent
He found her wandering on her own.
When asked if she had all things,
He the tree of life was shown.

She told him the words God uttered
About them both not eating fruit,
And how they both would suffer
And how He sounded resolute.
But the serpent laughed and told her
It was not possible they'd die,
They would become as wise as he was
Who lived in the heavens on high.

So, tempted, Eve succumbed to
All the words the serpent told.
Reaching high into the branches
She found a fruit and took tight hold.
Pulling down she gazed in wonder
Before she took a nervous bite
Standing there once she had eaten
She declared the serpent, he was right.

Then quickly finding Adam
She told him God was wrong.
Persuading him to follow,
Adam meekly went along.
They soon started feeling nervous
About what the Lord would say.
Making sure they both were hidden
When the Lord passed by their way.

God called out to His children,
And asked where they both were,
Wandering inside ever deeper
He found they both were there.
When asked why they were hiding,
Adam said they were afraid,
Ashamed as they were naked,
The Lord He felt betrayed.

Consumed with righteous anger,
The Lord to them decreed,
They would now both leave the garden,
Condemning all their future seed
Forever to be workers
But now with blisters on their hands,
Being torn by thorns and thistles
As they exhausted, ploughed their lands.

To Eve He was dismissive,
She was first of both to sin,
Proclaiming when in labour,
He would increase the pain within.
The serpent was not forgotten,
He would remember what God said,
He would sidle on his belly,
And man's heel would crush his head.

God then closed up the garden,
He sealed tight the entrance gate.
Although loving his created,
It was the sin that he did hate.
With man forever outside
Many tears have now been cried,
The day cast out from God's presence
Is when Adam and Eve died.

But God has not forgotten,
He knows we all will fail.
That's why he is our captain
As on the sea of life we sail.
If we continue on life's journey,
Believing in his precious son,
Repenting all of our failings,
He'll forget the wrong we've done.

A promise made to all men,
By the Father long ago,
Was for each man salvation,
Because he loves us so.
And on the day of judgement,
When our Lord returns again,
The faithful will be welcomed
In heaven where God does reign.

There gathered into heaven,
Are saints from times gone by
Gathered there because of Jesus
Who for each one did die.
He lived and taught amongst them,
Then crushed the serpents head,
Showing to all he was immortal
By rising from the dead.

Gods Plan

He has given us this earth,
The heavens he did display,
The darkness it was banished
He produced the light to give us day.
The seas the land and all the beasts
Which roamed upon this earth,
With many blessings he has given us,
From the moment of our birth.
Instead of thanking God on high,
For all that he has done,
Man, selfishly accepted all,
And crucified his son.

He promised Abram long ago,
A kingdom he would give
And all the tribes of Israel
In that promised and would live.
In time the promise came to pass
His word was true and sure,
His faithfulness was proven,
They could not ask for more.
Instead of thanking God on high,
For all that he has done,
Man, selfishly accepted all,
And crucified his son.

He cared so much for man he sent
His son to guide his flock.
But people turned their backs on him,
With derision they did mock.
They closed their eyes to all he said,
And chose Barabbas to be free,
Then took the holy son of God
Killing him on Calvary.
Instead of thanking God on high,
For all that he has done,
Man, selfishly accepted all,
And crucified his son.

There Jesus died so willingly,
He showed obedience to Gods will.
In piecing pain he cried aloud,
Then died upon that hill.
God still shows his love each day
On us blessings he does pour.
With a promise of eternal life
For all who do endure.
Instead of thanking God on high,
For all that he has done,
Man, selfishly accepted all,
And crucified his son.

Deliverance

God looked down at all His chosen, forced into labour by the sword,
Their cries reached up to heaven, praying they were not ignored.
Gathered in the dust bowl underneath the burning sun,
Israelites worked, pressured, to finish work they had begun.

Captured by Egyptian soldiers, fearful, powerful men of arms.
They were driven out of cities, and some evicted from their farms.
All were gathered and led onward, bound by shackles and by chains,
Until they reached the land of Egypt, where the Egyptian Pharaoh reigns.

Working constantly in sunlight, each day the hours were very long,
They prayed to their God in heaven offering up their mournful song.
They were slaves, they had no freedom, they were constantly in fear,
They shed blood and sweat like rivers, their eyes had shed many a tear.

They all believed their God would save them, rescue each man from their plight,
He would send someone to lead them, and if called on, they would fight.
The days morphing into weeks, and weeks morphing into years.
Had their God ignored their calling, had their God ignored their tears?

Then one day a man came preaching, telling all he'd lead the way
Into a land of milk and honey, they'd all be free one day.
They knew the man as Moses, once a favourite of the King,
Each slave became excited at the words that he did bring.

He just had to go to Pharaoh, and get him to release
The slaves and give them freedom, allowing all to live in peace.
Moses with his brother Aaron before the Pharaoh made request
To release all of their Gods children the ones he had repressed.

But the Pharaoh he did not listen, he refused to let them go,
There was work to finish in his kingdom, he needed those slaves so.
There was no way he'd make agreement not even if he could,
But Moses said filled with God's spirit said, "I'll turn your water into blood.

You will understand God's power, which exists in heaven on high,
You'll be unable to drink the water, all fish in the Nile will die".
And as God promised the once clean water, turned and clotted into blood.
But Pharaoh would not release them even if others thought he should.

Then Moses said the next plague would be frogs upon the land
Then Aaron brought frogs forward by holding his rod out in his hand.
But still the Pharaoh would not listen, he refused to let them go,
He would keep his slaves in bondage, he was unbending like his bow.

Then God said unto Aaron, strike your rod into the ground.
And when Aaron had obeyed Him, gnats from dust crawled all around.
Lice covered all the Egyptians and the livestock on each farm,
Each one felt pain and suffering, but the Israelites knew no harm.

Still the Pharaoh he was stubborn, God had hardened all his heart,
He would not release his captives, their journey out they would not start.
God brought forth swarming creatures which attacked both beast and man,
Pharaoh said he would release all, to fulfil part of God's plan.

They'd go when the plague was over, they would be free to leave his land,
But when God ended all the torment, Pharaoh dealt another hand.
He refused to free the captured, refused to let God's people go
He would not release one person, then God dealt him a further blow.

He sent a plague to Egypt on all livestock walking round,
Becoming sick each beast it suffered then fell dead onto the ground.
But the Israelites in Goshen they escaped all that befell
What had happened there in Egypt, just like the holy scriptures tell.

Pharaoh stood with his heart hardened, as death Egypt's beauty spoils,
His mind he didn't alter, then God sent a plague of boils.
Moses gathered soot from furnaces and released it from his hand
And boils covered Egyptian man and cattle, every creature in the land.

But Pharaoh still was stubborn, his heart was filled with ire,
So God sent another warning, this time thunderstorms of hail and fire.
God gave to them a warning to gather their beasts and livestock in,
For he would rain down hail and fire, the next day it would all begin.

He would demonstrate his power making tumult on earth below,
It was a sign that should be heeded, they were to let his people go.
But still the slaves stayed captured, enslaved by Pharaohs tightening hand,
God said if he would not release them, locusts would cover all of the land.

They would eat all crops left standing, and all trees that did remain,
Every person would be covered, each Egyptian would feel pain.
Although Pharaoh saw Gods power and all things that he could do,
He thought that he could beat Him, but Pharaoh hadn't thought it through.

God sent them days of darkness which covered every inch of land,
Three days they were in darkness after Moses held out his hand.
Finally, God gave an instruction to daub each captives house with blood,
For he would kill the all first born of houses which had no painted wood.

The first born of each family in all homes throughout the land,
Would be taken by deaths Angel, directed by Gods vengeful hand.
The cries and shouts were lifted, as each infant was deceased,
And as more and more were taken, the mournful sorrow sound increased.

This time Pharaoh feeling fearful that he was about to die,
"The Israelites, free them, release them", became was his fearful cry.
The Israelites all gathered and in haste they made their way,
Singing praises to their Father on their deliverance day.

There began an arduous journey of the people of the Lord,
Sometimes traveling unhindered, sometimes fighting with their sword.
After forty years of travel, they entered the promised land,
Guided, fed and watered by Gods almighty hand.

God was faithful to His people showing how much He loved them so
By changing Pharaohs standing when he let Gods' people go.
And then they started on their journey, into the promised land.
Guided by their savior, always fed and watered by His hand.

In Faith

Many years past giving birth,
Sarah heard God say,
Her barren time was soon to end
And she a son would bear one day.

Although she laughed, it came to pass
And Isaac he was born.
Oh, how her kin sang and rejoiced
On that momentous morn.

He grew up strong and knew his God
And praised Him every day,
And Abraham he was very proud,
But shocked at what God next did say,

He wanted him to prove his faith
By offering his son
As a blessed sacrifice,
And soon his journey was begun.

Into the hills by rugged track,
Father and son walked,
To offer God a sacrifice
Was by both the subject talked.

When they reached the chosen place
An alter they did build,
Abraham helped there by his son,
With dread and fear was filled.

Because Abraham trusted God,
The oath he made he'd keep.
Then Isaac asked if he should go
And find a sacrificial sheep?

But Abraham with a tearful eye
Explained what God had asked,
And how by faith he must complete
The job, which he was tasked.

So, Isaac climbed and laid flat down,
As his body Abraham bound,
Then offering prayers up to his God,
Fetched his knife from off the ground.

In faith the blade was lifted up
Above the very nervous boy,
Who was a glorious gift from heaven,
Bringing his parents so much joy.

Eyes closed tight the knife came down
Towards the young boys' chest,
Then God said "Stop, you've proved your faith,
By your side let your knife rest".

With so much joy the binds were cut
And Isaac clambered down,
They fell into each other's arms,
Smiles replacing Abraham's frown.

Then all at once a lamb appeared,
With pure white woolen fleece.
They offered up a sacrifice
And inside felt so much peace.

They offered up to God that day
A sacrifice of blood,
And God blessed Abraham and his tribe,
Just like He said He would.

And over time the tribe increased
As many as stars above
And those who walked in faith with God,
Were each day bathed in love.

By showing faith in God above
And trusting in His ways,
Abraham received God's favour,
And was blessed all of his days.

Realised

I was walking on a tightrope
Hovering above hells' flaming fire.
Living with depravity,
I felt no need to get much higher,
I fed my mind with evil
Until the darkness filled my soul.
Then I saw the light of Jesus
How his power could make me pure and whole.

Then I realised where I was and what I'd been,
Realised that his blood could wash me clean.
Realised my whole life had been all wrong,
Realised that he'd loved me all along.

So, I stopped what I was doing,
Rose above the depths of shame.
Set my mind upon the glory
I received through Jesus name.
Began to share with others,
All the good news of his word,
Prayed the Lord would reign forever
In the hearts of everyone who heard….

Prayed they'd realise Jesus died,
For souls unclean,
Realise he exists although unseen.
Realise that the scriptures are his word,
Realise just how much their saviour cared.

One day the earth will burn up,
Skies they will exist no more,
All the saved will rise and meet up
With the saints who've gone before.
All praising their redeemer,
Paying homage at his feet,
Saints from different centuries,
Recognising everyone they'd meet.

Then they'd realise it all had been worthwhile,
Realise as they enter Single file,
Realise as they see the streets of gold,
More beautiful than ever they'd been told.

Are you walking on a tightrope?
Hovering above above hells fire,
Living with depravity,
Feeling no need to get much higher?
Will you corrupt your mind with evil,
Until the darkness fills your soul?
Don't be blind to the light of Jesus
Allow his power to make you whole.

Faith and Works

I had a dream, if it was a dream,
In a room, I was all by myself,
I was glancing at the books I'd collected,
All resting there very high on the shelf.
Warm comfort was growing inside me,
As I was lounging stretched out by the fire,
Self-satisfied I knew I was successful,
Watching flames, flickering climbing higher.

I looked proudly at my treasure
Thinking everything I saw, I owned,
And wondered when cash would be collected,
From my brother to whom I had loaned.
I was drifting, so warm and relaxing,
There was nothing in my life to fear,
Watching each day my own wealth increasing,
My importance in life it was clear.

Then disturbed by a tap on the window,
And waking from my reverie.
Looking up, I saw a man's image,
Wondering who could that stupid fool be?
Surely anyone out there would be freezing,
In the snow pouring down from the sky.
Why would anyone think to disturb me?
Couldn't they just have kept walking on by?

I put down my mug on the table,
And decided I should take a look,
Reluctant, I rose from my comfort,
Begrudging each step that I took
To the window as I slowly went walking,
I looked out and the man that I saw,
Was a person I'd known for a long time,
Huddled, shivering outside my front door.

He was a friend, who had always supported,
My mentor I suppose, you could say.
Without his help I would truly be nothing
In the business world I live in today.
Why on earth would he think to come knocking,
He looks terrible, and in such acute pain,
I'll spare him a few of my moments,
Before I send him, on his way again.

False smile quickly was fixed on my visage,
Robe held tightly against my warm chest,
Wanting to see what was ailing my old friend
If needing help, surely, I'd do my best.
I said, "How are, you must be freezing?
Goodness me, you are looking so thin.
If it wasn't so near to my bedtime,
I'd have no hesitation in asking you in.

What is it I hear you are saying?
You are destitute, hungry and broke.
Your health truly has started to fail you,
Beginning when you first had your stroke.
You've no food to feed to your family,
You have no bread and you have no meat,
But things I'm sure will turn to better,
And soon you'll be back on your feet.

I'm sure you'll be able to find someone,
To sustain you with drink and some food,
Now it really is past my bedtime,
Please forgive me, I'm not being rude.
My night-time drink it is waiting,
On the table there, inside my cup,
I'm sure you be soon feeling better
And your life's fortunes, one day will pick up".

Closing the door, I left him there, standing,
Outside in the cold and snow.
Through the window, I stood, watched him turning,
Wondering wherever my old friend would go.
Standing there looking out of the window,
I saw him walking slowly away,
Of course, I would gladly have helped him,
If only he'd come here another day.

I have plans for all my money,
There's only so much I can spare.
If I gave it out to all and sundry,
My accounts would be empty and bare.
I had given my friend my best wishes,
Hoping things for him soon would improve,
I'll offer prayers up to heaven for him,
Asking his worries our God would remove.

As dreams do, I then travelled forward,
In another time, and another place,
As I looked around while I was standing,
I recognised a pale, friendly face.
My old mentor I stood watching him walking
Down the road with his wife by his side,
I felt shame, I felt really embarrassed,
But there was nowhere around I could hide.

As he walked he went up to a beggar,
I listened hard so I could hear,
He was asking my friend for some money,
My friend he had none, that was clear.
But what he did next, it surprised me,
He took hold of the beggars' left arm,
Lifting him up, ever so gently,
Promising he would come to no harm.

He said "My friend I don't have any money,
But I ask you please, don't think me rude,
If you accompany us to our lodging,
You'll be welcome to share some food".
The beggar looked and soon began smiling,
Eyes quickly turned and glanced over my way
I remembered that night, how I acted
And the words that I didn't say.

When my mentor the night he came knocking,
When he was truly in such terrible need,
I didn't offer to him any comfort,
I didn't invite him inside to feed.
I stood watching as they all went walking
Slowly towards my poor mentors' home,
I turned, hands pushed inside my pockets,
And walked away slowly, alone.

Their sound of their laughter it echoed,
As I travelled alone to my door.
Why was it with all of my riches
I had always been yearning for more.
My mentor, well he truly had nothing,
But it appeared he had much more than me,
A wife a home and much laughter,
How I longed to be happy as he.

As dreams do, I went to the future,
Beholding a bright throne of gold,
And a light of such brilliant whiteness,
Which was too glorious for me to behold.
I stood surrounded by people,
Some I'd known for numerous years,
Some were smiling and some they were joyful,
Some had eyes filled with terrible fears.

Then my mentor he came walking past me,
On his way onward towards the shining light,
His face was so clear and was beaming,
His smiling eyes were shining so bright.
He then entered in through the doorway,
To join all of the blessed within,
While others they all entered darkness
Cast aside due to their souls full of sin.

I asked of an angel there by me,
Why I had not been invited ahead,
"My friend" the Angel then whispered,
"Your place is to reside with the dead.
The others are going into heaven,
Their blessed existence to start,
They had a purity found in all of those
Who loved Jesus with all of their heart.

The Lord had blessed each of them daily,
And shown to them such gentle care,
Each of these souls, well, they were selfless,
Their blessings with others did share.
The sinful souls, those who are rejected,
And cast into the furnace of fire,
Had eyes only for their own pleasure,
Much too selfish to ever look higher.

Their desire it was concentrated
In only treasure found inside the world,
And because of their sinful intention,
Eternal death to them has been unfurled.
But you my friend, you have been given,
A chance, before your futures sealed,
And a vision of your looming judgement
Before that time, to you, is revealed.

The wealth and the treasure you've gathered,
In the life that you have lived on earth,
May be used for good things or evil
Your daily actions, well they prove your worth.
Remember you turned out your mentor,
Into the darkness and wet, freezing night,
With everything you have just learned now,
Your actions, tell me, were they right"?

I looked in shame at my companion,
Tears were streaming from both of my eyes,
The person over time I'd turned into
Was a person I began to despise.
I lusted for riches and money,
In things that eventually would fade and rust.
And if I want to join Jesus in heaven,
After righteousness my heart it should lust.

All at once, back to bed I then travelled,
And as soon as my body did wake.
I started reassessing my values,
For my eternal existences sake.
Evaluating of all of my riches,
And all of the money I had,
The selfishness existing in my life,
Was the reason I was lonely and sad.

Working hard I made full provision
For each person I knew was in need,
Giving money and aid to the homeless
To buy food on which they could all feed.
Then there at the home of my mentor,
I arrived in deep shame and disgrace,
I asked if he would ever forgive me,
As tears freely flowed down my face.

I told him I'd really been selfish,
My actions they had been so wrong,
Believing I'd been self-sufficient,
But mistaken I'd been, all along.
An alternative way now was open
Resulting in a change to my ways,
Enabling me to share all of my riches,
Helping others the rest of my days.

I know now that there is a treasure,
Eternal and will not rust or fade,
I told him of my warning vision
Which to my mind that night was relayed.
I then asked him to take time and teach me,
All the truth of Gods' heaven above,
And of Jesus, his gift of salvation,
His steadfast offer of eternal love.

Of the promise he offers to all men
To help them to all change their ways,
How he'll lead all believers to heaven,
Supporting and helping them all of their days.
I believe now my life is much richer,
As I study and learn of Gods' plan,
Appreciating all of his' blessings,
Sharing his love with my fellow man.

Be Careful

Don't walk down to destruction
Where the fallen, lost souls dwell.
And all those who rejected Jesus
Live eternally in Hell.
Don't fall for Satan's promise
Don't pay the price of sin
When Jesus comes in glory
And the saved hear "Enter in".
Be careful where you wander,
Be careful where you stay,
Walk the road that leads to glory
When Christ comes on judgement day.

Throughout life all weary travellers
Seek for paths to find their way,
Some travel through the night time
Some travel through the day.
Some don't seem to have a purpose
Aimlessly wandering around,
Unaware they have arrived or,
Their destination they have found.
Be careful where you wander,
Be careful where you stay,
Walk the road that leads to glory
When Christ comes on judgement day

We have one life to live here
On God's created earth,
And constantly he's called us
From the moment of our birth.
He is there to help and guide us,
And with love he's there to lead
Guiding and paying for our journey,
When Christ on the cross did bleed.
Be careful where you wander,
Be careful where you stay,
Walk the road that leads to glory
When Christ comes on judgement day.

One day you will be beckoned
To come and meet before your Lord,
When Jesus comes in glory
Holding high his spiritual sword.
Will you enter then in heaven
Or be cast down into Hell?
Will you live with him in glory,
Or in torment will you dwell?
Be careful where you wander,
Be careful where you stay,
Walk the road that leads to glory
When Christ comes on judgement day

Take Care

Take care when thoughts enfold you,
And temptation rears its head.
When enticement it beguiles you
To the place of all the dead.

Take care when you're deciding,
Which road you finally choose to take.
Is it the road that leads to heaven
Or God's grace will you forsake?

Take care when all your longings
Draw you deeper into sin.
And you spend your time ignoring
The spirits' voice, from deep within.

Take care when thoughts are closing
And the Lord is left outside,
For his day will soon be dawning,
There'll be no place left to hide.

Take care which cloak you're wearing,
As you walk this world of shame.
Know there is a cloak of blessing,
For all who call on Jesus' name.

Take care when you are living
A life, so full of spiritual pride
Knowing the evil one is waiting,
For a weakened soul to slide.

Take care, beware of danger,
That awaits those who are weak,
And turns them away from Jesus,
And worldly pleasures they all seek.

Take care beware of darkness,
Which tries to stifle Jesus' light.
Leading away the fallen,
Into a world of endless night.

Jigsaw

I placed the last piece in the jigsaw,
The picture was complete,
I admired the whole creation
It was a picture of our street.
I had no pieces over,
And none more were required.
I admired the colourful picture,
And thought the creator was inspired.

Then one day the family gathered
Around the picture lying there,
They looked with admiration,
Congratulations filled the air.
They looked at all the colours
And how each one blended in.
The people and the buildings,
The discarded rubbish in the bin.

They sat, and began discussing,
Whether if they could, enhance
The picture there before them,
I just watched them in a trance.
They removed one of the corners
Changing the shape that lay before,
It wasn't long before I noticed,
There were pieces on the floor.

Other pieces changed their colour,
Different shades contrasting hue,
It soon became apparent,
Those untouched, were only few.
Then more pieces they were added,
They were needed I was told,
In time the finished article,
Lay before us, clear and bold.

"Look that's nothing like my picture,
It has changed, it's not the same.
I know you all felt you were helping,
But it was treated like a game.
You thought you all knew better,
Don't disagree, I know you did,
But the jigsaw is much different
Than the picture, on the lid".

So, they turned and left the table,
Leaving the jigsaw lying there.
It was changed, out of proportion,
I fell deep into despair.
Then I thought about the Saviour
And the word He handed down,
The instructions there before us,
And His promise of a crown.

I thought about the changes
Made by man throughout the years,
Who discarded Gods instructions,
Saying "Truth only interferes".
Changing the plan, they all felt better,
It fitted in with modern life,
Making many alterations,
Like a surgeon with his knife.

But God said His word's unchanging,
It is now as was before.
There is no need for us to alter,
One iota, jot, or more.
He tells us that we should never,
Add any words or take away.
We only should take notice
Of what He alone, does say.

Mankind thinks that they know better,
They change, add, and take away,
They feel they can interpret,
What God really meant to say.
But the picture they are painting,
Differs greatly from Gods plan,
He is the one who drew the blueprint
Painting Salvations path for man.

Beware

Beware of the shining teeth,
Beware of the glinting eyes,
Beware of the silky words
Beware of the devils lies.

Evil watchers waiting for you
Wanting to beguile you and deceive.
Words of syrup hiding meaning
Sugar coating all their lies.
With ambition to ensnare you
Into their web of sinfulness.
Until they finally lead you
Into the place where your soul dies.

Shielding eyes restricting vision
Until you believe all that they show,
Controlling all your daily input
With all the power that that implies.
Wanting you to choose to follow
Willingly to give your heart
Until they finally lead you
Into the place where your soul dies.

Beware of all their power
Beware of everything they do,
Listen for other unfortunates
Who from the lost place raise their cries.
Be prepared to stand and counter
Each day be strengthened by Gods hand
Let His truth finally lead you
From the place where your soul dies.

Beware of the shining teeth,
Beware of the glinting eyes,
Beware of the silky words
Beware of the devils lies.

HOPE

Three Days.

At night deep in the garden
Midst the darkness, flowers and the trees,
A group of priests and soldiers came
A betrayed man to seize.
They'd devised a plan to take the one
Who preached Gods kingdom's close at hand.
He taught this message every day
As he travelled throughout the land.

First day into darkness
Second into rest,
Third day raised into glory,
The most holy and the blessed.

No matter how hard the priests had tried
They could not find a way
To snare or trap him with their words
They could not snare their prey.
And now they have him in their grasp
No more will he contradict
Their words and how they lived their lives
Their chance now to convict.

First day into darkness
Second into rest,
Third day raised into glory,
The most holy and the blessed.

He won't escape they told themselves,
We'll prove that we are right.
They bound and tied him, led him out,
Disciples fled into the night.
They ran away in total fear,
They abandoned Him who came
To save each sinner from eternal death,
By believing in his name.

First day in to darkness
Second into rest,
Third day raised into glory,
The most holy and the blessed.

Now hiding deep amongst the mob
Gathered before the governors' place,
Where they'd heard he had been brought
Followers strained to see his face.
Amidst a throng of noisy men,
They were pushed from side to side,
As they stood there waiting for their Lord
Some their faces tried to hide.

First day in to darkness
Second into rest,
Third day raised into glory,
The most holy and the blessed.

Bustling, shoving, straining their necks,
They saw the captured figure displayed.
The crowing and chanting easily led crowd
Had no idea they'd all been played.
The high priests in their vestments
And their staring, venom filled eyes,
Are vomiting words full of bile.
As they continued compiling their lies.

First day in to darkness
Second into rest,
Third day raised into glory,
The most holy and the blessed.

The abandoned accused, seemingly now all alone,
While a robe on his shoulders is laid.
Amongst all the rabble crying out for his death,
Are his silent followers, bereft and dismayed.
Oh, what now for them? Their leader is bound
A crown of thorns is placed on his head,
He is surrounded on all sides by faces of hate,
Each wanting to see their Lord dead.

First day in to darkness
Second into rest,
Third day raised into glory,
The most holy and the blessed.

Watching with tears running free from their eyes,
Afraid of what next is to come,
They hear all the words being thrown at their Lord
Scornfully mocking, priests treat him like scum.
Accusations are made he spoke blasphemous words,
Saying he was the true son of God.
They see him violently birched by the soldiers of hate
Watch as their spears his bruised body they prod.

First day in to darkness
Second into rest,
Third day raised into glory,
The most holy and the blessed.

"Prophesy if you are who you claim to be,
You will know who had struck you just then
But your silence condemns you, you have no idea,
You are the most deluded of men"
Pilate, he turned and washed both his hands,
Saying "I want nothing to do with this man,
Take him and punish him under your law,
I've done all that I possibly can".

First day in to darkness
Second into rest,
Third day raised into glory,
The most holy and the blessed.

But then Pilate was told of the custom,
Of releasing a prisoner, the crowd got to choose.
Then Pilate gave in, and decreed to allow
The crowd, their prerogative to use.
"Jesus or Barabbas" he asked of the crowd
Which man they would like to see freed.
The priests stirred for Barabbas and he won the vote.
And Pilate to them did concede.

First day in to darkness
Second into rest,
Third day raised into glory,
The most holy and the blessed.

"But what of this man, what should I do,
Beat him then cast him outside?"
But the priests' followers stood and stirred up the crowd
"Crucify" each one of them cried.
So, Pilate gave him to the charge of the priests,
Telling them he would not interfere,
"Just take him and deal with him as per your laws,
Take him, far, far away from here".

First day in to darkness
Second into rest,
Third day raised into glory,
The most holy and the blessed.

The Lord followed his cross to a hill outside the walls,
Known as Golgotha, the place of the skull,
The priests were so pleased to have captured their man
With pride they were gloating and full.
They gave him to soldiers saying "Do what you do,
This man he needs to die with the rest
Put him with the criminals all brought here to die,
He's yours, do what you do best".

First day in to darkness
Second into rest,
Third day raised into glory,
The most holy and the blessed.

Lying him down with his arms spread out wide
They secured his body with care,
They knew that all things must be secured and right
When lifting his cross in the air.
The nails pierced his flesh, on his hands and his feet,
His body hung high on the cross.
His followers stood watching with tears in their eyes,
Each one of them mourning their loss.

First day in to darkness
Second into rest,
Third day raised into glory,
The most holy and the blessed.

They watched as his last breaths were leaving his lungs,
Watched the priests and the soldiers walk by,
Then a loud cry emitted from the man on the cross,
" Eloi Lama Sabacthini"
"It is finished" he said then he gave up the ghost
And with a slow final bow of his head,
His followers knew as they took in the sight,
The man they had followed was dead.

First day in to darkness
Second into rest,
Third day raised into glory,
The most holy and the blessed.

The sky it went dark the curtain was torn
In the temple, the house of the Lord,
In a effort to ensure the convicted had died,
A soldier reached, pierced his side with a sword.
Blood and water flowed out together and mixed,
As a proof that their saviour was dead,
They forgot all, the things that their teacher had taught
They forgot all that Jesus had said.

First day in to darkness
Second into rest,
Third day raised into glory,
The most holy and the blessed.

Some disciples came forward His body to claim,
Asking to take it with them to a tomb.
Where they'd bind it with cloths till the Sabbath was o'er
When their anointing they would then resume.
His body was laid in a new unused tomb,
Loaned by Joseph of Arimethia,
Then a stone was rolled to cover the mouth
And a battalion of soldiers stood near.

First day in to darkness
Second into rest,
Third day raised into glory,
The most holy and the blessed.

The priests were afraid his followers would steal
His body, and hide it away,
Telling all that the Lord had been true to His word,
He had died but rose on the third day.
Soldiers were placed at the mouth of the tomb,
Ensuring nobody could come and try
To steal the body, and continue to preach
What their saviour said wasn't a lie.

First day in to darkness
Second into rest,
Third day raised into glory,
The most holy and the blessed.

Now happy the body was safe and secure,
The priests went on their way to prepare
To tell all the people that Jesus had died,
Now he'd gone they'd no worry or care.
The people they all now would listen to them
Again, their prestige it would grow.
The false-prophet was gone, no one now to deflect
Their teachings, how they hated Him so.

First day in to darkness
Second into rest,
Third day raised into glory,
The most holy and the blessed.

During sabbath disciples they followed the law,
Each portion they did all obey.
Still thinking of what had become of their Lord,
Not considering the words he did say.
Then the Sunday arrived, the first day of the week,
The women, they all were prepared,
To visit the tomb start anointing the one
Who had died, but for whom they still cared.

First day in to darkness
Second into rest,
Third day raised into glory,
The most holy and the blessed.

On the way Mary asked, "But what of the stone,
Will there be someone to roll it away?
Allowing us to enter and put balm on our Lord,
Let a strong person be there let us pray".
When the women arrived, the stone had been moved
And Mary in fear entered in,
To see if the body was still there inside,
So their anointing they could then all begin.

First day in to darkness
Second into rest,
Third day raised into glory,
The most holy and the blessed.

On stepping inside she noticed a form,
It was a figure standing there dressed in white.
An ethereal glow was all around him,
A shining and brilliant pure light.
"The person you seek, the one that you want,
Is risen, your Lord is not here,
He told you his body would rise up again
In a message he made it so clear.

First day in to darkness
Second into rest,
Third day raised into glory,
The most holy and the blessed.

"Remember the message he preached to you all
After experiencing death he would rise,
After offering himself as a sacrifice
He showed the way to his home in the skies".
Then Mary amazed, turned and walked away
Her heart rejoicing although full of fear,
Then a voice she heard nearby and recognised,
Calling her name, it was gentle and clear.

First day in to darkness
Second into rest,
Third day raised into glory,
The most holy and the blessed.

"Master" she cried in joy falling down
Worshipping right there at his feet.
Her saviour was standing, raised from the dead,
Her happiness now was complete.
"Go tell the others" she heard her Lord say,
"I will visit with each one of them soon.
Tell them they'll all see me when I appear,
Amongst them all in the upper room".

First day in to darkness
Second into rest,
Third day raised into glory,
The most holy and the blessed.

Mary ran quickly retracing her steps
To tell the disciples of all that she saw.
Her feet moving fast she soon covered the ground,
Not stopping until reaching the door.
"The Lord he has risen, I've spoken to him,
The masters alive he's not dead".
The disciples all thought that she'd lost her mind,
Grief had caused sickness, deep inside her head.

First day in to darkness
Second into rest,
Third day raised into glory,
The most holy and the blessed.

But she continued to speak until each of them heard
The words she was bursting to say,
Then Peter, James and John all rushed out
With renewed hope they with joy made their way.
Arriving they found his body was gone,
Mary was sane she had not lost her mind.
The linen once wrapped around his face and his form,
Were the only things the disciples could find.

First day in to darkness
Second into rest,
Third day raised into glory,
The most holy and the blessed.

On returning again to the upper room,
They shared with all, the things they had seen,
They told of finding the funeral cloths
In the place where his body had been.
Gathered together they sang their hymns and they prayed,
Until amongst them the Lord did appear,
He told them He'd send them a comforter
A helper to make all things for them clear.

First day in to darkness
Second into rest,
Third day raised into glory,
The most holy and the blessed.

"Carry the message into all of the world
And preach each day of what is to come.
Tell everyone how they can all get to heaven
Baptised and believing in God's only son".
The message was preached the seed it was sown,
Many people from that day have been saved.
They have all entered heaven while leaving behind
A sinful world and souls lost and decayed.

First day in to darkness
Second into rest,
Third day raised into glory,
The most holy and the blessed.

Three days it was from the death our Lord,
Until His body in power it was raised.
Giving each sinful man the chance to receive
Salvation for all, Christ be praised.

The Day of the Lord

How I long for the day of the Lord,
When all shall see His face.
And those who have believed in Him,
Shall find shelter in his grace.

Oh, that great and powerful day,
When the earth and old heavens will all pass away,
And sin and death will be no more,
The saved gathered there on new heavens shore,
Oh, that great and powerful day,
When the old earth and old heaven pass away.

How I long for the day of the Lord,
When there at his feet we will fall,
And all will find a welcome there,
Who listened and answered Jesu's call.

Oh, that great and powerful day,
When the earth and old heavens will all pass away,
And sin and death will be no more,
The saved gathered there on new heavens shore,
Oh, that great and powerful day,
When the old earth and old heaven pass away.

How I long for the day of the Lord,
When in new heavens land we will stand,
Walking with him through the streets filled with gold
Guided by our loving Saviours' hand.

Oh, that great and powerful day,
When the earth and old heavens will all pass away,
And sin and death will be no more,
The saved gathered there on new heavens shore,
Oh, that great and powerful day,
When the old earth and old heaven pass away.

How I long for the day of the Lord,
To see him appearing once more in the sky,
Gathering all the saints of earth to him,
To live there with him by and by.

Oh, that great and powerful day,
When the earth and old heavens will all pass away,
And sin and death will be no more,
The saved gathered there on new heavens shore,
Oh, that great and powerful day,
When the old earth and old heaven pass away.

Another Day

Another day begins,
I will gather with my friends,
We will fly around together in the sky.
Our daily chorus we will sing
As we honour God our King,
Who watches over us from the heavens way up high.

Have faith, have faith in Him your saviour Christ who died,
Have faith, have faith in God's blessed son the crucified.
Who rose, who rose and over death claimed victory
To show, to show that we from sin can all be free.

Everywhere we look
In the field or in the brook,
There is food that is just waiting to be found.
Rain water cures our thirst,
Not too much or we could burst.
We find lots of blessings scattered all around.

Have faith, have faith in Him your saviour Christ who died,
Have faith, have faith in God's blessed son crucified.
Who rose, who rose and over death claimed victory
To show, to show that we from sin can all be free.

We don't toil or work the land,
All is provided by Gods hand.
Everything we need is there and more besides.
As we fly around all day
We know he guides us on our way
Watching over us from Heaven where He resides.

Have faith, have faith in Him your saviour Christ who died,
Have faith, have faith in God's blessed son the crucified.
Who rose, who rose and over death claimed victory
To show, to show that we from sin can all be free.

But the ones who share this earth
Born in His image from their birth.
Seem to live their lives immersed in stress and strain.
Filled with worry toils and woe,
They on life's journey doubt filled go.
Forgetting they have a God to ease their pain.

Have faith, have faith in Him your saviour Christ who died,
Have faith, have faith in God's blessed son the crucified.
Who rose, who rose and over death claimed victory
To show, to show that we from sin can all be free.

Faith size of a mustard seed
Is all anyone would need
To tell a mountain to be lifted out to sea.
If they have faith in God above,
They would experience His love
As from their turmoil and despair He sets them free.

Have faith, have faith in Him your saviour Christ who died,
Have faith, have faith in God's blessed son the crucified.
Who rose, who rose and over death claimed victory
To show, to show that we from sin can all be free.

If for the birds He does provide
Clothes them makes them full inside,
How many blessings to His children will He give?
To each one He offers life
Unburden them from sin and strife,
Offering all a home in heaven where they can live.

Have faith, have faith in Him your saviour Christ who died,
Have faith, have faith in God's blessed son the crucified.
Who rose, who rose and over death claimed victory
To show, to show that we from sin can all be free.

Their loving saviour knows they're weak,
And if to Him they turn and speak,
He has promised He will never let them down.
And for all those who walk HIs way
Praising Jesus everyday
There waits for faithful ones a Heavenly crown.

Have faith, have faith in Him your saviour Christ who died,
Have faith, have faith in God's blessed son the crucified.
Who rose, who rose and over death claimed victory
To show, to show that we from sin can all be free.

He Will Be There

When darkness falls, and it blackens your way,
Chasing the brightness from your day,
Just call on Him, He will answer your call,
Just call on Him, He's the saviour of all.
And know that,

He will be there, to guide you along,
He will be there, to help you be strong,
He will be there, you're not on your own,
He will be there, you're never alone.

When friends are few, and you feel alone,
And you just feel so far from your home,
Just call on Him, He will answer your call,
Just call on Him, He's the saviour of all.
And know that,

He will be there, to guide you along,
He will be there, to help you be strong,
He will be there, you're not on your own,
He will be there, you're never alone.

When burdens are great and you're feeling tired,
You've don't have the strength that is required,
Just call on Him, He will answer your call,
Just call on Him, He's the saviour of all.
And know that,

He will be there, to guide you along,
He will be there, to help you be strong,
He will be there, you're not on your own,
He will be there, you're never alone.

When the time comes, for you to leave,
And your final state is there to retrieve,
Just call on Him, He will answer your call,
Just call on Him, He's the saviour of all.
And know that,

He will be there, to guide you along,
He will be there, to help you be strong,
He will be there, you're not on your own,
He will be there, you're never alone.

"Who will roll away the stone?"

"Who will roll away the stone?"
Mary to the others said,
"Who will roll away the stone?"
Mary to the others said,

"Maybe the soldiers will roll it away"
Mary to the others said.
"Maybe the soldiers will roll it away"
Mary to the others said.

But when they got there, the tomb was bare
The stone was rolled away.
An angel told them "He is not here
Your Lord has risen today".

The disciples they did not believe
They just had to go and see.
The disciples they did not believe
They just had to go and see.

When they got there His body was gone
But they did see where He did lay
A man in White said "His body has gone
Your Lord has risen today".

So off they went their hearts in song
And met Jesus on the way,
Falling at His feet they bowed their heads
Listening to what their Lord did say.

"Go into the world and preach the word",
Jesus to his disciples said.
"Tell them how much their saviour cared",
Jesus to his disciples said.

"Tell them their sins can be forgiven",
Jesus to his disciples said.
"Tell them their saviour from death has risen",
Jesus to his disciples said.

And when they got there, the tomb was bare
The stone was rolled away.
An angel told them "He is not here
Your Lord has risen today",

He Is Not Here

He is not here the women cried,
As they reached the tomb and looked inside,
No body there where He did lay
When they laid him down late in the day.
The women had made plans to pour
Lotions on his form, so purged and sore.
His body had been hung up high
Upon a cross, left there to die.

They searched the tomb looking for their Lord,
Whose side was cruelly pierced with sword.
They asked where they had taken him,
So their embalming they could begin.

Oh, how they watched with tearful eyes
As the one they loved was crucified.
They listened as soldiers scorned their Lord
And watched one pierce him with a sword.
Then as water with blood flowed from His breast,
They knew then that he had entered rest.
They gently took his body down,
To a vacant tomb outside of town.

They searched the tomb looking for their Lord,
Whose side was cruelly pierced with sword.
They asked where they had taken him,
So their embalming they could begin.

The tomb belonged to another man
Who said he'd do whatever he can
And help them take care of their Lord,
Whose breast was so cruelly ripped by sword.
They carried their Christ so carefully,
Longing once more, his smile to see
To hear again how he was sent by God,
And how he descended from Jesse's rod.

They searched the tomb looking for their Lord,
Whose side was cruelly pierced with sword.
They asked where they had taken him,
So their embalming they could begin.

But now he's gone no corpse to see
Oh where, could their messiah be?
Then an Angel said, "Be not afraid,
From death your Jesus has been raised.
He'd followed through his Fathers' plan
Offering eternal life to every man.
Be patient and wait, he will return,
He's conquered death, eternal life now yearn".

They searched the tomb looking for their Lord,
Whose side was cruelly pierced with sword.
They asked where they had taken him,
So their embalming they could begin.

Soon Christ in body did appear,
Told his disciples to have no fear.
Reminding of the time when he had said
In three days he would raise from the dead.
He said go out and preach the word,
Tell people how much their saviour cared,
And how their sins would be forgiven
By their loving Father who reigns in heaven.

They searched the tomb looking for their Lord,
Whose side was cruelly pierced with sword.
They asked where they had taken him,
So, their embalming they could begin.

In the upper room where they had seen their friend,
On them the Spirit it did descend,
Filling them with strength of faith and power,
They walked streets and preached, that very hour.
No reason now, to run and hide,
The Holy Spirit they had inside.
They preached how sins could be forgiven,
By their saviour who had returned to heaven.

They searched the tomb looking for their Lord,
Whose side was cruelly pierced with sword.
They asked where they had taken him,
So their embalming they could begin.

The word has spread the whole world wide,
Telling of Jesus crucified,
And how he rose up from the dead,
Fulfilling all things the scriptures said.
He's promised one day he will return,
And for that day our souls should yearn,
To see him appearing in the sky,
His word is truth, he does not lie.

They searched the tomb looking for their Lord,
Whose side was cruelly pierced with sword.
They asked where they had taken him,
So their embalming they could begin.

We shall not know when he'll appear,
Or when the Angels song we'll hear.
He'll come to call the faithful few,
Leaving one alone where there once was two.
Just like a thief who works at night,
No warning of their coming plight.
So be prepared, alert and true,
When He returns, he'll be judging you.

They searched the tomb looking for their Lord,
Whose side was cruelly pierced with sword.
They asked where they had taken him,
Their embalming they could begin.

They missed Him so he was their friend
He told of love that will not end.
He spoke of things they did not know,
He was their Lord, how they missed him so.
But soon their sorrows all were gone,
They preached of him the blessed one,
They told how a crown of life awaits
For all the saved through heavens gates.

An empty tomb, and his body gone,
Was proof that Jesus he was the one,
Sent down to earth by our God above
A sacrifice to show us His love.

No searching now all has been revealed,
God's love by Jesus, it has been sealed.
His word is truth, Jesus does not lie,
He waits for us far beyond the sky.
No fear of death, eternal life for all,
Who are faithful to their saviours call.
When you hear his word, don't turn him down
You'll reject the chance of a heavenly crown.

An empty tomb, and his body gone,
Was proof that Jesus He was the one,
Sent down to earth by our God above
A sacrifice to show us His love.

When He Returns.

There'll be people giving praise
When he returns.
It'll be the end of days
When he returns.
On their knees they'll all fall down
While the Lord awards their crown,
They'll be glad they changed their ways
When he returns.

The seas will give up all their dead
When he returns.
Corpses will rise like Jesus said
When he returns
Gathered by the judgements seat,
Kneeling down before His feet
Each their saviour they will meet,
When he returns.

Some will have crowns put on their head
When he returns.
Some others hearts will fill with dread,
When he returns.
It is then they'll realise
There is a home beyond the skies,
But they'll be cast out with the dead,
When he returns.

Will you find eternal rest
When he returns?
Will you enter with the blessed
When he returns?
Or will you join with those in hell
Who had fallen under Satan's spell,
Not called to be their saviours' guest
When he returns?

How Long?

How long, how long, will we have to wait?
How long, walking the pathway so narrow and straight?

"Where I am going you cannot come"
Words spoken by the blessed son,
"You see me now, but soon no more,
Until you enter heavens' door.
Believe my words and follow me,
From deaths cruel sting you will be free,
I am the last, there are no more,
Believe in me, my words are sure".

How long, how long, will we have to wait?
How long, walking the pathway so narrow and straight?

For three short years he preached the word
Of how our Heavenly Father cared,
Telling all the depth of our Father's love
Sent down to earth, from Heaven above.
Although nobody ever could find blame,
They said he had no right to claim
That He and our God above are one,
They devised a plan to have Him gone.

How long, how long, will we have to wait?
How long, walking the pathway so narrow and straight?

By bribing one with evil heart,
Their plan to kill they soon would start.
Deceiving people with their lie,
The crowd they shouted, "Crucify".
Upon a hill our saviour died
"Our Lord is dead", disciples cried,
But from despair they soon would turn
When his victory over death they'd learn.

How long, how long, will we have to wait?
How long, walking the pathway so narrow and straight?

Our saviour told them of the plan,
To preach God's word, to every man.
How reward in heaven waits for those,
If the straight and narrow path they chose.
He told them one day all will see
Him appear again in victory.
And all the saved will rise up high
To live with Him 'neath Heaven's sky.

How long, how long, will we have to wait?
How long, walking the pathway so narrow and straight?

Welcome Home

I fell asleep one evening,
Dreams floating through my head
And the one that I remember
Is the dream where I was dead.
Amongst so many people
Far as the eye can see
Then I heard my saviour say to me,

I heard him saying "welcome home",
I heard him saying "welcome home",
He took hold of my hand
Led me to the promised land.
Saying "blessed pilgrim welcome home".

He told me I'd been faithful
My love for him I'd shown,
Each day while striving to be good
He'd seen my faith had grown.
He said my race had finished
No running anymore,
And then my saviour opened heaven's door.

I heard him saying "welcome home",
I heard him saying "welcome home",
He took hold of my hand
Led me to the promised land.
Saying "blessed pilgrim welcome home".

Then suddenly I woke up,
Still wrapped up in my bed.
But all the sights I'd dreamed of,
We're so clear inside my head.
I knew where I was going,
The things that I must do,
To get to heaven, to Him I must be true.

And hear him saying "welcome home",
And hear him saying "welcome home",
He'll take hold of my hand
Lead me to the promised land.
Saying "blessed pilgrim welcome home".

We a Will Rise

We will rise into the sky, when Jesus comes
In all his glory,
Gathered by His throne, thankful we believed
Salvations story.

Walking the streets of gold, marvelling at the sights
That fill our mind,
Not thinking of the world that we've just left,
So far behind.

We will meet with all the saints when we arrive
And recognise,
No strangers will we meet recognition we will see
Inside their eyes.

Walking the streets of gold, marvelling at the sights
That fill our mind,
Not thinking of the world that we've just left
So far behind..

Such glorious sights will our minds absorb,
We'll comprehend.
As we marvel at the sights which fill our life
Which has no end.

Walking the streets of gold, marvelling at the sights
That fill our mind,
Not thinking of the world that we've just left
So far behind.

A promise made to those who walked with God
In days gone by.
When we're raised by Christ our Lord the blessed Son,
Who came to die.

Walking the streets of gold, marvelling at the sights
That fill our mind,
Not thinking of the world that we've just left
So far behind.

When he rose he promised he would come again,
To judge us all.
He's prepared and shown a way we can escape
From Adams fall.

Walking the streets of gold, marvelling at the sights
That fill our mind,
Not thinking of the world that we've just left
So far behind.

Like a thief comes in the night, he will return,
So be prepared.
You'll have no defence if you ignore
The news you've heard.

Walking the streets of gold, marvelling at the sights
That fill our mind,
Not thinking of the world that we've just left
So far behind.

Meeting Jesus.

I have travelled on this weary road,
By friends I've been betrayed,
Made mistakes along the way
Which in love my God forgave.
I've battled against evil,
Had darts fired at my soul,
But I kept my faith in Jesus,
The one who's made me whole.
But now my time has ended,
My journeys at an end.
I'm going to meet Jesus,
My saviour and my friend.

Precious Jesus lift my soul up,
Let me take hold of your hand.
Today I will meet Jesus,
My saviour and my friend.

I'll walk along with Jesus,
And with him at my side,
I'll meet all of the saints who
Were faithful when they died.
They stood against the darkness,
And fought the evil foe,
Putting on the gospel armour,
As onward they did go.
Now gathered all together,
Receiving their reward
Bathed in all the glory
Of their redeeming Lord.

Precious Jesus lift my soul up,
Let me take hold of your hand.
Today I will meet Jesus,
My saviour and my friend.

By My Side

I wonder at your love for me,
The blessings that you give.
I wonder at your faithfulness,
And how you help me live.
Each day I see your bounteousness,
Your blessings all around.
But why do I deserve these Lord,
When my feet trip on the ground?

I look at how I've treated you,
And how I've let you down.
But still you hold your hand to me,
With the promise of a crown.
Your arms are wide and long to hold,
My spirit deep within.
But constantly I let you down,
And wallow in my sin.

Still you are there to comfort me
And support me when I fall,
You never turn your face away,
Or ignore my pleading call.
I let you down so often Lord,
I pierce your wounded side.
I constantly ignore you Lord,
While basking in my pride.

When I take time to look around,
At all the gifts you give.
I know that you are always there,
To instruct me how to live.
Your depth of love I can't compute,
I just can't understand,
How you can see me daily sin,
Yet still hold out your hand.

You are the most amazing thing,
To have happened to us all.
Always ready, waiting for
Our assistance needed call.
You do not judge us when we sin,
You do not turn away.
You don't want one soul to fail,
But to be saved on judgement day.

I love you Lord with all my being,
My soul, my life, are yours,
Please help me to be worthy of
Your love that Christ ensures.
Without you we would have no hope,
Without you we are not here.
But with you Lord, against Satan's power,
We have nothing to fear.

Please help me Lord to give my all,
Please help me to obey
The rules of love you demonstrate,
And follow them, each day.
I am, a lost and lonely soul,
If you're not by my side,
I pray you'll make my heart your home,
Let your spirit inside abide.

Please cleanse my soul, and cleanse my mind,
My thoughts and words control.
I want you to take all of me,
Please Father, make me whole.
Forgive me for the sins when I,
Unwittingly do fail,
And grieve the one who loves me most,
He who waits behind the veil.

I want to shine with Jesus' light,
In the darkness of this world.
I want to tell of Jesus' love,
And how to all it is unfurled.
I give my life, my all to you,
To count all things as naught.
I want to follow in the way
Our saviour Jesus taught.

Please help me Lord, you are the one
On whom I can depend.
I'll never know a deeper love,
Or know, a dearer friend.
All I have you give me Lord,
And all I have is yours.
But your greatest gift there waits for me
With you on heavens shores.

Then I will see your glorious face,
And to you in praise, bow down.
It's there you will present me with,
Your promised, heavenly crown.
Please help me Lord to walk your path
Each day, please help me love
And praise you Father, Lord of Hosts
Who reigns in heaven above.

I give my life, my heart, my all
To you, to use and lead,
Please help me to obey you Lord,
And on your scripture, daily feed.
The evil one lays traps for me,
To cause my soul to stray,
But I know I am not alone,
You're with me every day.

You give me strength to fight the foe,
Preach your word, throughout the land.
And if I slip or drop my guard,
I know, you'll understand.
Our life goes on, but then one day,
This shell our souls will leave,
A heavenly crown waits for all
The saints, who did believe.

I am your slave O blessed one,
I am at your command.
To go, wherever you may lead,
Across this sinful land.
I know, with you I will not fail
With your spirit as my guide.
I can go forward, marching on,
With you there at my side.

We'll Walk with Him.

We'll walk with him,
We'll walk with him,
We'll walk with him, one day,
When he returns
From where He is,
We'll walk with him on that day.

He's promised us,
He's promised us,
He's promised us a home,
When he returns,
From where he is,
We'll enter our promised home.

His word is sure,
His word is sure,
His word is sure always.
When he returns
From where he is,
We'll walk with him all of our days.

He does not lie,
He does not lie,
He does not lie, He's pure.
When he returns
From where he is,
We'll be with him for evermore.

He sent his son,
He sent his son,
He sent his son, to die,
When he returns,
From where he is,
We'll live far beyond the sky.

Do you believe,
Do you believe,
Do you believe in him,
When he returns
From where he is,
We'll be cleansed from all our sin.

Give him your heart,
Give him your heart,
Give him your heart today,
When he returns
From where he is,
We'll walk with Him on that day.

Maranatha

Maranatha our Lord come,
Maranatha blessed Son,
Maranatha King of Kings,
Maranatha the saints all sing.

Oh, Holy Father, the woes of life
Churn the hearts of struggling souls.
They allow themselves to be led away
As despair their life enfolds.
But those of faith who walk the path,
That Jesus trod before,
Look to heaven and call for him,
To open heaven's door.

Maranatha our Lord come,
Maranatha blessed Son,
Maranatha King of Kings,
Maranatha the saints all sing.

The promise you gave in ages past,
To those who loved you Lord,
To protect and care for faithful souls,
Whose hearts sing with one accord.
And who do not lust for worldly things,
Only desire for things above.
Your faithfulness you've shown to them,
And your constant steadfast love.

Maranatha our Lord come,
Maranatha blessed Son,
Maranatha King of Kings,
Maranatha the saints all sing.

We long to see your wonderful face,
And worship at your feet.
To reside in our heavenly home,
Recognising all we meet.
Though these are things we long for Lord,
The timings in your hands,
Please hear the words as in one voice,
Saints sing throughout the lands.

Maranatha our Lord come,
Maranatha blessed Son,
Maranatha King of Kings,
Maranatha the saints all sing.

Shining light

There'll be a shining light,
Coming down from way up high.
There'll be a shining light
Coming down from way up high.
When our saviour returns,
We will see Him in the sky.

Praise him, praise him, praise him our precious Lord,
Praise him, praise him, praise him, our precious Lord.
He died for us on the cross
To let us share in his reward.

Angels singing His praise,
When our saviour comes again.
Angels singing His praise,
When our saviour comes again.
Gathered there by His throne,
Singing glory to His name.

Praise him, praise him, praise him our precious Lord,
Praise him, praise him, praise him, our precious Lord.
He died for us on the cross
To let us share in his reward.

All the scriptures they warn,
We are in the end of days.
All the scriptures they warn,
We are in the end of days.
But if we love and trust Him,
He will be our God always.

Praise him, praise him, praise him our precious Lord,
Praise him, praise him, praise him, our precious Lord.
He died for us on the cross
To let us share in his reward.

Will you rise with the saved,
Or be found amongst the lost?
Will you rise with the saved,
Or be found amongst the lost?
Accept salvation its free,
Our saviour He has paid the cost.

Praise him, praise him, praise him our precious Lord,
Praise him, praise him, praise him, our precious Lord.
He died for us on the cross
To let us share in his reward.

Praise him, praise him, our precious Lord,
Praise him, praise him, our precious Lord.
Our salvation is sure,
And we can share in his reward.

We Are Special

We are special, we have a father full of love.
We are special, a promised home for us above.
We are special, God has provided everything.
We are special, lift up your heart, be glad and sing.

There is a promise,
made to all, in days gone by,
Made by our Father,
who lives in heaven, above the sky,
It is a promise,
that He's made to everyone,
Who'll choose to follow,
and believe, in Christ His son.
He has loved us,
from before our very birth.
Knowing our value,
our Father knows our very worth.
And if we take time,
to read all the scriptures say,
About how Jesus,
how He'll return to us one day.
He will then judge us,
judge every soul who's walked this Earth,
Welcoming all those,
who have experienced spiritual birth.
Those who rejected,
the offer of our faithful Lord,
They will be cast out,
and will receive their just reward.
There in the darkness,
they will all weep and gnash their teeth,
Loudly they'll cry out,
pleading and begging for relief.
But those who loved Him,
those who believed in all He said,
How He was beaten,
how He was crucified 'till dead.
How on the third day,
His tomb was empty and was bare,
His binding linen,
and His face cloth lying there.
Now resurrected,
appeared to women and to men,
And those who loved Him,
began to preach His word again.
It was all for us,
He wants nobody to be lost,
No need to purchase,
for our Lord has paid the cost.
Because He loves us,
and His loving has no end,
He is our Father,
He's our eternal, loving, friend.

That's why we're special, our Saviour calls to everyone,
He wants to take us, into the place where he has gone.
He has a mansion, for every soul who takes his hand,
Letting him lead them, into the blessed promised land.

At the Feet of Jesus

We'll be wearing crowns upon our heads
As we walk the streets of gold
Our eyes will look in wonder
As the treasures all unfold.
We'll sit at the feet of Jesus
And see His shining, wondrous face,
Immersed inside the beauty
Of His eternal grace.

At the feet of Jesus, gathered 'round His golden throne,
Singing praises with the Angels, in our eternal home.

The world with all its troubles
Wears each lowly pilgrim down.
As they strive along the highway
Leading to their golden crown.
Each day the Lord of evil
Tries hard to tempt them from the way
Which leads to eternal glory,
Theirs when Christ returns one day.

At the feet of Jesus, gathered 'round His golden throne,
Singing praises with the Angels, in our eternal home.

Close at hand the Saviour's waiting,
For the call from His beloved,
With His hands outstretched and reaching
To support those he has loved.
He offers respite from the peril
From the sins that lead to harm,
Leading all his blessed homeward
Guided by His loving arm.

At the feet of Jesus, gathered 'round His golden throne,
Singing praises with the Angels, in our eternal home.

When we're there we'll meet with people
Who once walked this earth before,
We'll gather with those pilgrims,
Over there on Heavens shore.
We'll sing praises to our Father,
Who for us, sacrificed His son,
Him who was by His side in heaven,
Before history had begun.

At the feet of Jesus, gathered 'round His golden throne,
Singing praises with the Angels, in our eternal home.

In All His Glory

There will come a day when this earth will end,
And heavens and stars will pass away.
When the Lord in glory returns again,
To judge each soul on judgement day.
All the lost will run, attempt to hide away,
They know they're heading for a fall.
They all had their chance but they rejected Him,
Who offered grace and life to all.

Appearing with His angels
He'll light up all the sky,
His trumpet sound will be loud and clear.
Gathering the blessed
Into their heavenly home,
Embracing those who had loved Him dear.

All the saved will walk there with their loving Lord
In lands so pure and free from thorns.
A shining light pure and brighter than the sun,
With love each day their soul it warms.
They will live in peace, no sadness will they feel,
No pain or sorrow fills their mind.
Happiness and joy, and pure eternal bliss,
God's love each pilgrim there will find.

There in all His glory,
They'll be gathered 'round His throne,
Angels and cherubim's sing his praise.
Saints from many ages
All welcomed to their home,
Living in heaven with Him always

There will no more be temptation to sin,
No more will evil fill their soul.
They are living with the blessed crucified,
Whose risen spirit made them whole.
Prepared for each a mansion up in heaven
For all those faithful to the Lord,
Who through all their lives and struggles fought the fight
Armed only with God's spirits sword.

Armed only with God's spirits sword.
They joined the army of their Lord.

GODS' LOVE

Ransom Paid with Love

Satan looks around each day
Surveying the world before,
He looks for those who've lost their way
And ignore Salvations door.

His evil finger wrapping tight,
Around the poor, lost souls,
Draws them deep into his power,
Until each morsel he controls.

He looks for those, who close their ears,
And love each part of self.
No thought, for their eternal souls,
Or their state of spiritual health.

How tempting are his evil ways,
How sweet it is to sin,
Deflecting each desire to hear,
The Lords voice from within.

He tempts them all with earthly wealth,
Power and greediness are king.
To win no matter what the cost,
They must have everything.

They stand on all those in their way,
In search of their success.
They push their way out to the front,
They want more and more not less.

His net is wide, it gathers up
Lost souls drifting, all round.
He leads them to his dreadful lair,
Where pain and hate abound.

In Satan's lair they'll find no peace,
No hope, no love, no rest,
No satisfaction for those who,
His deceptions do digest.

Collecting all his prisoners,
Who do willingly concede,
Following him down the path to hell,
Satiating worldly greed.

They'll realise, they've followed lies,
They'll realise, that they were wrong,
When Christ appears in victory,
And they hear Salvations song.

Until we draw our final breath,
And we finally close our eyes.
We have the choice to walk the path
To where, salvation lies.

It's not too late to hear the call,
From Him who reigns above.
Who paid the price to cleanse our sins,
Our ransom paid with love.

He Gave His Son

Showing the depth of his love, He gave his son.

On his throne above the skies,
Where pure love and peace abides,
Our Father reigns on high, in his celestial home.
He's created all we see,
Gave us land amongst the sea,
With everything he's given to us, His love he's shown.

The time which was once prophesied
When his son was crucified
After finishing all that was to be done.
Suffering death for you and me
From our sin he set us free,
Showing the depth of his love, he gave his son.

On Calvary's hill he bowed his head.
The third day rose from the dead.
And proved he had the power to overcome all things.
His throne is high above the world,
Salvations banner now unfurled,
He is our Lord of Lord he is our King of Kings.

Angels gather round his feet,
Where saints from ages meet,
Singing praises there to the holy one,
Living with him eternally
From sins hold have been set free
Showing the depth of his love, he gave his son.

Showing the depth of his love, He gave his son.

Cradled in My Sweet Saviours Arms

Cradled in my sweet saviour's arms,
Cradled in my sweet saviour's arms,
Whenever I feel weak,
I know it's Jesus I should seek,
And I'll be cradled in my sweet saviour's arms.

When I find myself attacked each day from all sides
As Satan tries to reel my soul to him,
I just fall down on my knees,
And I offer up my pleas,
To the one who died and saved me from my sin.

And I'll be cradled in my sweet saviour's arms,
Cradled in my sweet saviour's arms,
Whenever I feel weak,
To I my saviour I just speak
And I'm cradled in my sweet saviour's arms.

When Gods son, Jesus lived and walked on this earth,
Preaching to each one to mend their ways,
He told them they were lost
And that he has paid the cost,
Being there to watch and keep them safe always.

And they'll be cradled in their sweet saviour's arms,
Cradled in their sweet saviour's arms,
Whenever they felt weak,
To their saviour they could speak
And they'd be cradled in their sweet saviour's arms.

Don't despair if the world seems tired and weary,
And everything you do is going wrong,
Just believe that up above
Is a saviour, who is love,
And who wants to guide you as you walk along.

And you'll be cradled in your sweet saviour's arms,
Cradled in your sweet saviour's arms,
Whenever you feel weak,
To your saviour you just speak
And you'll be cradled in your sweet saviour's arms.

Jesus Death and Crucifixion.

Kill him, kill him, the people cried.
To Pontius Pilate who stood beside
The Christ, the one who was betrayed,
By Iscariot for earthly gain.
Kill him, kill him, the shout was loud.
And Pilate, gave in to the crowd.
He washed his hands, and turned away
And gave Jesus up for pain.

The soldiers laughed and mocked the Lord.
Tormenting him with word, and sword.
A crown of thorns they pushed on him.
And watched the blood run free.
The soldiers, on their knees did fall,
They spit on, scourged him, one and all
They pushed Him round and slapped his head.
Acting brave for all to see.

The Saviour stood without a word,
Watching those souls, for whom he cared.
And for whom he'd come to die,
Do Satan's evil deed.
He took the vitriol and hate,
Knowing for them, it was not too late
As it was all part of The Fathers plan
And all that he had decreed.

Upon a cross, they hung him high,
Though body wracked, never a cry
Of condemnation, from his mouth,
He knew what he must do.
Then He finally hung his head,
"It's finished", is what our Saviour said.
It was then, He gave up his soul,
He died for me and you.

The skies went black, the curtain torn.
The afternoon, like early morn,
The rocks they split, and the dead were raised.
And the earth it shook that day.
Centurions standing, saw the sight,
As afternoon turned into night,
"This surely was the Son of God".
A soldier was heard to say.

The priests and Pharisees were scared,
"He'll rise again", is what they'd heard.
The temple he would build again,
With Him, the foundation stone.
Deep in a tomb they laid our Lord,
Protected by the soldiers' sword
In case disciples His body took,
And claimed for Him the throne.

The third day came, and Mary went
To tend the Lord, with oils and scent.
They were concerned for His earthly state,
Not understanding what he had said.
When they got there, they looked inside,
No body there and no place to hide.
Then an angel said, "please do not grieve,
He's risen from the dead".

For forty days the Christ appeared
And grieving hearts, He quickly cheered,
No longer did they feel unease,
But joyful, renewed love.
He walked with them, he drank and fed.
It's time to leave our Saviour said.
On a mountain high, they watched Him rise,
To take His place, in heaven above.

But quickly how the strength grows weak,
A place to pray they all did seek,
To ask for strength to fight the foe,
And do the Saviours will.
One day praying, they all in one place,
The Spirit arrived lit every face,
It filled them all, revealed its truths,
Their hearts they couldn't still.

So off they went and preached the word
About how Jesus truly cared.
How through Him they'll have eternal life,
And how for everyone He'd died.
Hear, believe, repent and be baptised
He's the only way, they emphasised.
To enter into the Fathers place,
And share the glories that wait inside.

It falls on each to make a choice
To follow Him, and then rejoice,
Or turn and sadly choose the world
The realm of the evil one.
Till He returns, His promise stands.
To everyone throughout the lands.
Eternal glory is there for all,
Who follow, Gods Heavenly Son.

Mansion in the Sky.

One day while walking down the street
A friend of many years I chanced to meet,
He looked and said to me "My you look tired"
I told him from my job I'd just been fired,
I had no hope, there's nowhere I could go,
He looked at me and said, "That is not so,
There is a golden place prepared for all,
Who follow God and answer Jesus' call",

There is a mansion in the sky,
Prepared for all the saints from times gone by,
Where those blessed souls who've chosen love
Can live in peace with God in heaven above
There is a mansion on the sky.

I said that is no help to me right now,
I have no work, no field to plough,
How can I find food and clothes to wear?
I've asked many people, they just don't care.
Tell me where's my future where's my hope,
I don't want to end my life on a dangling rope?"
But he said "My friend please don't despair,
There is love around us in the air",

There is a mansion in the sky,
Prepared for all the saints from times gone by,
Where those blessed souls who've chosen love
Can live in peace with God in heaven above
There is a mansion on the sky.

He said "If you have faith in God above,
He will furnish all because of love,
The birds don't worry where they'll find food,
God's love to them each day is proved.
All the grass and flowers in fine array,
Show the world their beauty every day,
He provides for them, how much more He will give you?
Have faith in him, His word is true.

There is a mansion in the sky,
Prepared for all the saints from times gone by,
Where those blessed souls who've chosen love
Can live in peace with God in heaven above
There is a mansion in the sky.

Pentecost

It started with an empty tomb,
And men huddled in an upstairs room.
Unsure of what they next will do,
They had many foes, but they were few.
Three days now since their master slain,
In a borrowed tomb, His body lain.
Then came loud knocking on the door,
And hurried feet across the floor.
A story told so breathlessly
Of His body not, where it should be.
The swaddling clothes were all in place,
Except the cloth that adorned His face.
They told of seeing two men there
With shining face and golden hair.
Saying the one they sought had gone away,
He was not dead, He had risen that day.
Then Mary said the Lord she saw,
As she looked passed the open door.
She said it's true, the Lord appeared,
He was not dead as they all feared.
The next forty days the Lord did walk
And appeared to many, to eat and talk.
Then the time came for His return,
To His heavenly home for which He did yearn.
He promised them that He would send,
A comforter their fears to end.
Then back to the room from whence they'd come,
They bowed their heads and prayed as one.
Matthias was chosen to take the place
Of the traitor Judas who'd found his place,
In a field he'd bought with his evil gains,
A field now cursed with his bloody stains.
While deep in prayer, they heard a sound,
Like a roaring wind which blew around.
It was the promised one that Jesus sent,
They were told to teach all to repent.
Filled with the spirit they all went down
To the market place in the bustling town.
They preached of Jesus and how He cared,
And though different tongue, each person heard.
Amazed they listened to what was said,
Of how God raised Jesus from the dead.
Heart broke, they cried "What shall we do?",
"Repent be baptised He'll forgive you".
Three thousand souls were saved that day,
Then rejoicing in Christ, went on their way.
That was the day, Christ's church was born,
Strong steadfast men, no more forlorn.
They preached God's word to far and wide,
No longer weak, no need to hide.
They told the truth where're they walked,
Where people where they stopped and talked.
They spoke from scriptures, stood their ground,
No variance from God's truth was found.
God's word's the same, it will not change,
Although men sometimes rearrange,

To suit their needs, they lie and bend,
The truth and Salvations plan amend.
Despite God saying His word is sure
And shall be constant evermore.
No need to add or take away,
From the message preached that fateful day.
Still men they try and search for proof,
What was preached that day, was not the truth.
They dispute God said in times gone by
He'd send His son for us to die.
And He'd die by hanging on a cross,
Forgiving sins by His blood loss.
They try so hard and yet they fail,
For against Gods word they won't prevail.
Satan daily plants his evil seeds
Seducing his own to do his deeds.
They walk amongst us every day,
Decrying what our Lord did say.
They say Gods word is just a fable,
That He'd stop all wars if He were able.
He'd stop the suffering all around,
And when we die, our home is the ground.
They laugh and jeer those who believe
That Christ their burdens will relieve.
But their fate will be the same
As Satan and those who play his game,
Outer darkness, tears and pain
For those who sold their souls for earthly gain.
But for faithful ones He's said there's room,
For those who accept the empty tomb
Accepting that Christ rose from the dead,
And followed the words that Jesus said.
In heaven a place awaits for all
Who are faithful to the gospel call,
And obey His teaching every day,
Walking the straight and narrow way.

LIVING

It Is Written in His Book.

It is written in his book,
It is there, just take a look.
The pilgrim searching for the truth,
Will find it in his book.

We are told, there are so many ways,
To find eternal rest.
So many people try to show
Which way for us, is best.
But surely there is just one way,
Which isn't twisted by some crook.
A truth, which stands above them all,
And it is written in his book.

It is written in His book,
It is there, just take a look.
The pilgrim searching for the truth,
Will find it in his book.

Some people think it is good to add,
And some to take away,
From things we find inside Gods' word,
And from things, the Christ did say.
But the truth is flowing through His word,
Like a sparkling babbling brook.
If we open our hearts and search we'll find,
It is written in his book.

It is written in his book,
It is there, just take a look.
The pilgrim searching for the truth,
Will find it in his book.

The wisdom we find inside His book,
And the spirits guiding hand,
Will help us read what is in Gods word
And help us understand.
If we're sincere to follow His way,
Our sins He'll overlook.
There is no other way to find the path,
It is written in His book.

It is written in his book,
It is there, just take a look.
The pilgrim searching for the truth,
Will find it in his book.

Get Behind Me Satan.

Get thee behind me Satan,
You're standing in my way,
You won't divert me Satan,
From the straight and narrow way.
Putting on the gospel armour,
Will help protect my soul,
And fellowship with Jesus,
Will keep me pure and whole.

Satan get behind, get behind.
My soul in wretched sin you cannot bind.
Jesus, He died on Calvary,
From sinful chains to set me free.
My hope and faith in Him are thus entwined.

No matter how you tempt me,
I know I must stay strong,
And God's spirit will support me,
As He's promised all along.
You know my weakness Satan,
You know the reasons I could fall,
But I now have a protector
Since I answered Jesus' call.

Satan get behind, get behind.
My soul in wretched sin you cannot bind.
Jesus, He died on Calvary,
From sinful chains to set me free.
My hope and faith in Him are thus entwined.

He is my strength and anchor
In this world of storms and war,
He will encourage and protect me,
Shield me from your will and more.
Each day my communication
With my Father and my Lord,
Will bring me ever closer to him,
And reinforce my spiritual sword.

Satan get behind, get behind.
My soul in wretched sin you cannot bind.
Jesus, He died on Calvary,
From sinful chains to set me free.
My hope and faith in Him are thus entwined.

The things you offer Satan,
The temptations that you sow,
Will lead me to destruction
If onward, down your road I go.
But my God, he asks for nothing,
He only wants my love,
And he's promised me salvation
With him in heaven above.

Satan get behind, get behind.
My soul in wretched sin you cannot bind.
Jesus, He died on Calvary,
From sinful chains to set me free.
My hope and faith in Him are thus entwined.

You've naught to offer Satan,
Which will lead me from his way,
If I have faith and love Him
By my side he'll always stay.
His promise has been faithful
Throughout the realms of time,
There is no need for me to doubt him,
To his will, I will resign.

Satan get behind, get behind.
My soul in wretched sin you cannot bind.
Jesus, He died on Calvary,
From sinful chains to set me free.
My hope and faith in Him are thus entwined.

You've chosen your path Satan,
It's not the path for me,
While eternal hell you suffer,
Living in Heaven with him I'll be.
Listening to all the angels,
Lifting voices up in praise.
To God in all His glory,
Who reigns forever and always.

Satan get behind, get behind.
My soul in wretched sin you cannot bind.
Jesus, he died on Calvary,
From sinful chains to set me free.
My hope and faith in him are thus entwined.

Wanted high Up Yonder.

Wanted high up yonder,
In a place above the sky.
Where gathered in a land of love,
Are saints from times gone by.
After living lives so faithful,
And calling on the Lord,
They faced the devil, made him run,
From their blessed, spiritual sword.

It is a place, where untold wealth
And riches, can be seen.
Where hunger never rears its head
All souls are strong, not lean.
They're feeding on the bread of life,
It's sustenance fills all.
Their spirit strengthens every day,
Nothing now, can make them fall.

To each one who walks on this earth
A choice is clearly given,
To follow in the steps of him
Who, from his death was risen.
Or follow, in the steps of one
Who from the heavens was cast out.
To lead astray each living soul,
By lying, and sowing doubt.

He offers riches here on earth,
And teaches men to cheat.
He shows them how to kill and maim,
Mistrust everyone they meet.
He blinds their eyes, and hardens hearts,
Deceives them Gods truth, to reject.
And teaches, for God's written word,
They should have no respect.

He fills their minds with impure thoughts,
Encourages them to act
In ways that are unnatural,
While inhibitions they retract.
All the while, he moves around,
On his stomach he will slither
And although he promises lasting wealth,
He knows he can't deliver.

Deceiving Eve so long ago
With fruit from off that tree,
He promised they'd be wise like God,
And from ignorance be free.
That day they'd be his equal,
And His knowledge, they would share,
But God found them in the garden,
And cast both of them from there.

He told them they had all things,
And from need they would be free.
The only stipulation was
Not to eat fruit from off that tree.
But Satan he'd deceived them,
Telling lies, so clear and plain.
Now thrown out of the garden,
They could not enter back again.

Their lives now they were different,
Having to toil and till the earth.
And pain it was increased for Eve,
When she to a child gave birth.
They could have remained faithful,
They could with God have walked
With Him, there in the garden,
They could each day have talked.

But weakness and temptation
Brought punishment on all.
Because they heeded Satan's guidance,
After listening to his call.
They sought to be Gods' equal,
They thought they could be like Him,
So, they listened to the serpent,
And committed the first sin.

Satan working through the ages,
He has swindled and deceived.
Causing many to be stranded,
Because his word, they all believed.
His main purpose is to gather
As many souls, as he can reap,
Not revealing if they follow,
For eternity they'll weep.

But to us our Lord is calling.
He wants no single soul be lost.
His charge to us is nothing,
Because Jesus paid the cost.
He offers life eternal,
To all who do believe.
And to those who remain faithful,
A crown of life they'll all receive.

Christ said there is a mansion
Prepared and waiting up above,
For all those of His children
Who have given Him, their love.
He said the time is coming,
When all we see will disappear.
As we see Jesus reappearing,
And His judgement we all hear.

A new heaven and earth created
And new bodies we will wear.
And for the saved who followed Jesus,
There'll be a blessed welcome there.
But all those who followed Satan,
Will be all waiting about,
Then be thrown in outer darkness
As from Gods presence they're cast out.

All you travellers who are wandering,
Over God's created earth,
Take some time to have a listen
To Him, who's called you from your birth.
Take time to read the scriptures
Consider what will your choice be,
Will you live in outer darkness?
Or in Heaven eternally?

The Tongue

It is easy so easy to deceive people,
And lead some men astray with only words.
Diverting the pathway of searching,
Their foundations they shake and disturb.

No physical strength is required,
To alter a weak pilgrims way.
Just a word from that part of our body,
Can cause a faltering pilgrim, to sway.

Our tongue is a muscular organ,
Well-hidden operating alone,
But although in appearance it's harmless,
It has strength, which can shatter, a bone.

One word from our tongue can prove fatal,
And when carelessly used can be dire,
All the forest of civilisation,
Can be consumed in a tongue inspired fire.

A tongue that is useful in greeting,
Can cut very deep, like a knife.
A tongue can speak words full of feeling,
Or break the heart of a loving' young wife.

A tongue can speak such words of comfort,
To sooth and disperse all life's woes.
And a tongue can be used to greet people,
Or reject them when insults it throws.

Can a fig tree bring forth grapes or apples?
Can a stream have salt water and pure?
Can your tongue speak of God and of His kingdom,
While it tells lies, deceives people and more?

Be careful when using this muscle,
It can be sharp like a warrior's sword.
But it can have a wonderful usage,
When spreading the word of the Lord.

When He Returns.

There'll be people giving praise,
When he returns.
It'll be the end of days,
When he returns.
On their knees they'll all fall down
While the Lord awards their crown,
They'll be glad they changed their ways,
When he returns.

The seas will give up all their dead,
When he returns.
Corpses will rise like Jesus said,
When he returns.
Gathered by the judgements seat
Kneeling down before his feet
Each one their saviour they will meet,
When he returns.

Some will have crowns put on their head
When he returns.
Some others hearts will fill with dread,
When he returns.
It is then they'll realise
There is a home beyond the skies,
But they'll be cast out with the dead
When he returns.

Will you find eternal rest
When he returns?
Will you enter with the blessed
When he returns?
Or will you join with those in hell,
Who had fallen under Satan's spell,
Not called to be their saviour's guest,
When He returns?

Troubled Beings

She looks long into the mirror
And she can only sit and stir,
At the vision of perfection,
She sees reflected, there.
The journey wasn't easy,
It came at no small cost.
To achieve this heavenly body,
It was worth the pounds she'd lost.

As a child she was an ogre,
Perceived in her closeted mind.
So she started out on her journey,
And perfection, attempted to find.
She's a vacuously, bland person,
Immersed in gossip that she daily reads,
Reading all tips there on beauty
While on her insecurities it feeds.

There are, so many people, who
Look at the outward shell.
Holding up self-image as an idol
As lies to themselves, they tell
About their radiant beauty,
Glittering like the stars up above,
How they'll attract pure adoration,
And from lesser mortals, love.

But deep inside each human carcass
Is a soul, unloved, ignored?
It's existence, not deemed important,
To those so self-assured.
No thoughts for the final journey,
Each one of us must surely take,
While some ignore its sheer existence,
Making, such a big mistake.

Our bodies will all crumble,
Age will ravage mortal bones,
And the last vestige of our beauty
Will be an image on our phones.
Our souls before the Father,
Will make our last impassioned plea,
To be admitted into heaven,
And in His presence forever be.

Concentration on earthly beauty,
Will be shown to have been in vain.
And will be inconsequential
When Christ returns again.
Then he will separate each person
According to how he's seen them live
To some a place in outer darkness,
To others a home in paradise he'll give.

The Lord was questioned whilst on earth
By the priests and Pharisee,
With outer garments adorned, so all
Their importance they can see.
But the Lord saw deep in their heart,
And revealed their hypocrisy,
And said when Gods kingdom comes again,
If unchanged, outside they will be.

Just take care of who you are,
And just who you're trying to be.
Look for the beauty found deep inside
Follow Christ and be set free.
Dead men's bones and unclean souls,
Hidden from the public view,
Pretending to be pure within,
Troubled being, is it really you?

Time

You plan your trips so well,
No stone is left unturned,
Your spending fund you swell,
It's yours: it's what you've earned.
Each move is planned with care,
There's nothing left to chance,
You've borrowed for your fare,
You're in vacation trance.

Our eternity it starts the first beating of our hearts,
This beating it goes on until the power to beat is gone.
Our spirit leaves this shell, destination heaven, or may be hell?
Our home it is our choice, cower in dark or in light rejoice?

You check the doors are locked,
Make sure no villain can break in,
Access to all is blocked,
Possessions all secure within.
Your holiday's a week,
Although you really wanted more,
A rest is what you seek,
Well that's what holidays are for.

Our eternity it starts the first beating of our hearts,
This beating it goes on until the power to beat is gone.
Our spirit leaves this shell, destination heaven, or may be hell?
Our home it is our choice, cower in dark or in light rejoice?

All those many tiring days,
You've spent making all your plans
Stress your face displays,
You're sure no one understands.
Now your work is at an end,
You're ready to begin,
Excitement your best friend,
Starts with a tingling from within.

Our eternity it starts the first beating of our hearts,
This beating it goes on until the power to beat is gone.
Our spirit leaves this shell, destination heaven, or may be hell?
Our home it is our choice, cower in dark or in light rejoice?

You've done everything that you can
All boxes ticked and more,
Its time to fulfil your plan
Of sunbathing on the shore.
You've been given so much grief,
From the transient things of life,
All you want is some relief
From the rigours of your life.

Our eternity it starts the first beating of our hearts,
This beating it goes on until the power to beat is gone.
Our spirit leaves this shell, destination heaven, or may be hell?
Our home it is our choice, cower in dark or in light rejoice?

But leisure's value doesn't last,
Treasured memories soon are lost,
Hidden deep within your past,
As you try to meet the cost.
On life's' treadmill you do plod,
Ignoring just what is to come,
No time to think of God
And our saviour Christ His son.

Our eternity it starts the first beating of our hearts,
This beating it goes on until the power to beat is gone.
Our spirit leaves this shell, destination heaven, or may be hell?
Our home it is our choice, cower in dark or in light rejoice?

When you finally close your eyes,
And your spirit does depart,
Will it be peace beyond the skies,
Or will terror fill your heart?
Will all thoughts of wasted time,
And of values that were wrong,
With doubts will they entwine,
Was your time worthless all along?

Our eternity it starts the first beating of our hearts,
This beating it goes on until the power to beat is gone.
Our spirit leaves this shell, destination heaven, or may be hell?
Our home it is our choice, cower in dark or in light rejoice?

The time is here for you to think,
Of your life span here on Earth,
How you have teetered on the brink,
From the moment of your birth?
Your life's clock goes on ticking,
The fingers, keep on moving on.
But the pendulum stops its swinging,
When your last tick is gone.

Our eternity it starts the first beating of our hearts,
This beating it goes on until the power to beat is gone.
Our spirit leaves this shell, destination heaven, or may be hell?
Our home it is our choice, cower in dark or in light rejoice?

When you read your masters word,
Or hear a sermon taught,
Do you think of how God cared
And how our souls from sin were bought,
When He made the sacrifice
For us by sending down His Son,
Prepared to pay the final price,
Dying, when His work was done?

Our eternity it starts the first beating of our hearts,
This beating it goes on until the power to beat is gone.
Our spirit leaves this shell, destination heaven, or may be hell?
Our home it is our choice, cower in dark or in light rejoice?

Do you think of how the tomb,
On the third day it was bare,
And though they looked around the room,
Their messiah was not there?
Angels voices spoke quite plain,
Declaring Jesus Christ was raised
And that He'd return again,
To be worshipped and be praised.

Our eternity it starts the first beating of our hearts,
This beating it goes on until the power to beat is gone.
Our spirit leaves this shell, destination heaven, or may be hell?
Our home it is our choice, cower in dark or in light rejoice?

You only have to look around,
To observe His awesome power,
How His blessings they abound,
Every moment of each hour.
The promises God made,
To all men who do believe,
From death they would be saved,
He'd them from the grave retrieve.

Our eternity it starts the first beating of our hearts,
This beating it goes on until the power to beat is gone.
Our spirit leaves this shell, destination heaven, or may be hell?
Our home it is our choice, cower in dark or in light rejoice?

Scriptures tell of men who truth loathing,
Like wolves will creep right in,
Being disguised wrapped in sheep's clothing,
They'll lead the weaker men to sin.
Perverting truth and telling lies,
Profess to all that they know best,
The spirits word they will despise,
Jeopardising their eternal rest.

Our eternity it starts the first beating of our hearts,
This beating it goes on until the power to beat is gone.
Our spirit leaves this shell, destination heaven, or may be hell?
Our home it is our choice, cower in dark or in light rejoice?

All their teachings will be blurred,
From the church who at the start,
Were so faithful to the word,
And from the truth did not depart.
Weaker men will be confused,
Who then the true path they will leave,
Following lies in meetings used,
By the men sent to deceive.

Our eternity it starts the first beating of our hearts,
This beating it goes on until the power to beat is gone.
Our spirit leaves this shell, destination heaven, or may be hell?
Our home it is our choice, cower in dark or in light rejoice?

We will watch and raise our voice,
When the Saviour does return,
The saved will then rejoice,
The lost for solace they will yearn.
Will you rejoice, or will you cower,
Will you worship Him with praise,
Or be dread filled in that hour
Banished to darkness all your days?

Our eternity it starts the first beating of our hearts,
This beating it goes on until the power to beat is gone.
Our spirit leaves this shell, destination heaven, or may be hell?
Our home it is our choice, cower in dark or in light rejoice?

We are instructed to make time,
To understand the Saviours word,
Which tells of love sublime,
Tells us of just how much He cared.
Let us make sure we prepare,
For the time we leave this earth,
To absorb all Gods sensations,
Glowing in our spiritual birth.

Our eternity it starts the first beating of our hearts,
This beating it goes on until the power to beat is gone.
Our spirit leaves this shell, destination heaven, or may be hell?
Our home it is our choice, cower in dark or in light rejoice?

Acceptable Worship?

She says, "I must go to the meeting,
Everybody will be there.
Are my clothes all clean and tidy?
Do I need to wash my hair?
I will give my shoes a polish
I must have them shining bright.
Then they will be reflecting
When I'm standing in the light.
I have lain awake for hours
Planning what clothes I am to wear.
They must all be coordinated,
I must iron each one with care.
I cannot walk around with creases,
What will the others say?
I'll be given the once over
When I walk into church today.
Will they notice this thread hanging?
Oh, what am I going to do?
I cannot wear this grey now,
I must change and wear the blue.
The time is going faster,
Have I really time to change,
Should I repair this thread that's hanging
Or my outfit rearrange?
Oh, what a big dilemma,
My mind will just not be at ease
I must look appealing,
And each eye I've got to please.
Although it's late, I've changed now,
The time has come to leave.
My outfit is pure perfection,
The smartest there I do believe.
The clouds are looking heavy,
I just pray it doesn't rain,
For it will only spoil my outfit
And I cannot change again.
The wind will not stop blowing,
Disturbing my hat, my hair,
Which I've spent much time arranging,
And I've taken so much care.
At last I'm at the building,
I must go and take my seat,
It's right by the radiator
There I'll warm my hands and feet.
It's been my seat for years,
I've never sat elsewhere,
Right behind the Dolan sisters,
Such a prim and proper pair.
Is anybody looking?
This hat it is brand new,
I bought it for my grey coat,
But it goes just as well with blue.
The service is nearly ended,
Just one more hymn to sing,
I must be ready with my money
When, the collection plate they bring.

I hope they are all looking,
For I put in quite a lot,
I can't show I can't afford it,
Willingly given, I'll say it's not.
There at last the meeting's over,
I think I've made the grade.
Now I will go and have a listen,
To all the rumours being relayed.
"Well, I never knew that,
Did she really! What's she like?
Fancy claiming from the social
When her husband went on strike?
You'd think she could have managed,
How could she stoop so low?
The shame and indignation,
From our group she'll have to go".
It's time to return home now,
I am the last to leave.
I've listened to the gossip,
I've done my bit, I do believe.
Nobody can reproach me,
I've done my best and shown my face,
Proved I'm above the others,
Showing I can last the pace.
Well I'm home, I can relax now,
Store my bible 'till next week,
Still pristine after these years,
Maybe one day inside I'll peak.
But not right now, I'm just too hungry,
And my dinner I must cook.
I may have some spare time later
To open the book and have a look.
The speaker he looked tired,
Such a droning, boring voice,
How can such a morbid person,
Encourage each one to rejoice?
I just couldn't listen to the message
For which he'd studied and prepared,
It was probably just an old one,
One I had already heard.
I wish he'd write a new one,
Then to listen I'd be Inspired,
But I wonder if he's able,
And should he be retired?
Still, I know everything about it,
There's nothing I can be told,
I've attended many years,
In the warmth and in the cold.
I'm a much-respected person,
It's not me that should pay heed,
To a man who tried to give me
Much more scripture, than I need.
Of course, I believe in Jesus,
In the good book and its' tale,
But you know it's only written
For all the other ones who fail.
In my life, I am contented,
With the good things that I do.

I'm much better than the others
Everybody knows it's true.
I make sure, I tell the others,
Making sure, that they all see,
What's the use of doing good things,
If no credit comes to me?
Without me, the place would crumble,
Without me, things would not get done.
I am such a busy person,
With lots and lots of things to run.
I'm such an important person,
I'm loved I'm sure, by all.
I'm perfect, sure and steadfast,
There's no chance that I will fall".
Yes, with her life she's happy,
She gets praise, she gets respect.
She gives no credit at all to Jesus,
What from Him can she expect?
An empty shell existing,
Striving for the praise of men.
But when she stands in judgement,
What to her, will happen then?
Jesus standing in the temple
Saw a widow all alone,
Standing near an important rich man
And by his clothes his wealth was shown.
He was proud and showed to others
The amount of cash he gave.
Thinking he would get to heaven,
From burning hell, his wealth would save.
But the widow gave one penny,
It was all that she did own,
Jesus said by her contribution,
Her love to God that day she'd shown.
By giving from the pittance
On each day she did survive,
Her soul would be rewarded,
Eternally she'd be alive.
But the rich man he had plenty,
And each day craved the praise of men,
He had missed the point of giving
But he had time to learn again.
God gives us many blessings,
And all of these we do not own,
So, let us take and share with others,
Following the example he has shown.

Conscience.

Well that worked out well didn't it?
You thought you just knew what to do.
Many times, you've made plans in your head,
Now you've had the courage to see the act through.

Now, whatever went wrong with your plan?
The tablets and booze you laid out,
The bottle of vodka was large
It would work, you were never in doubt.

Tell me, where are you my clever one?
Experiencing peace, you dearly sought?
Is it tranquility the place you are in now,
Or is it in limbo that you are now caught?

Eyes closed you look like you are dead now,
But your chest keeps on moving in, out,
As your lungs fill with air then dispel it,
And your lips have a permanent pout.

You're still aware of many noises,
And the voices unclear to your ears,
Are all muffled but echoing loudly,
Compounding the depth of your fears.

The sound of loud beeping machines
Recording each beat of your heart.
And blood pressure pads record pulse and,
If and when your improvement does start.

Blurred spectral ghosts pass by your eyes,
Closed eyelids distorting their form.
Like clouds they pass aimlessly on,
Floating dancers, for you, they perform.

Aware of her hovering nearby,
You long to have words with the nurse.
But your incapacity to make any sounds,
Makes it difficult for you to converse.

Death you thought would end all your woes
And your troubles you'd leave all behind
But instead you're reliving them each hour
As the images flood into your mind.

So where next for you floundering friend,
Can you leave while still strapped in your bed?
Are you condemned to pointlessly fade,
While listening to me in your head?

Lying here in your hospital room,
I'm the one voice you will clearly hear.
The one who said no at the time,
But you ignored me, wanting to be freer.

I am trapped my dear friend so are you,
Both of us, we have nowhere to go.
What you've done has diminished us both,
No opportunity now for us to grow.

As long as your body takes breath,
Possibly years for you lie ahead.
Lying here in your hospital room
You'll regret every hour you're not dead.

But never fear my suffering friend,
I am sure you will soon understand
You are living in this state of hell
Brought on your own careless hand.

No movement and no voice to speak,
All because you thought you knew what's best,
Well with me in your head my trapped friend,
You will not get one moment of rest.

So, prepare for long hours of remorse
Expect many, years of regret.
A winning hand you thought you did hold,
My misguided friend, you have just lost your bet.

Your torment will go on and on
Until the Lord puts an end to your pain.
You'll stand there before Him on His throne
Patiently waiting for you to explain.

TEACHING

First Will Be Last

A vineyard owner surveyed his land,
With a satisfied smile said, "This looks grand",
The vines are thick and heavy with fruit,
For harvest help, I'll make pursuit.

So off he went down to the square,
To choose from labour, standing there,
And willing to work for one whole day,
One denarii agreed would be their pay.

After a time, he looked around,
And much more fruit could still be found.
Then at the third hour he did return,
With an offer of pay labourers could earn.

The sixth, and ninth, and eleventh hour,
He returned, idle labourers to empower.
After agreeing that he would see them right,
They carried on working until the night.

The time arrived to receive their pay,
First in line were those, who worked all day.
In front of those they were before,
And expecting to be paid much, much more.

But finding all were paid the same,
It appeared to some an uneven game.
One denarii paid to one and all,
On the vineyard owner they went to call.

"You're paying them what? That's just not right,
We've worked from dawn until the night.
Our hands are cut and more bugs in our hair,
If you ask us master, it's just not fair".

But the owner said, "Why bother me,
On one denarii' did we not agree?
My friend I did not do you wrong,
I've treated you fairly all along".

"Please take the wage I promised you,
I'll give to them what I gave to you.
All I have belongs to me,
Do you begrudge my generosity".

Jesus spoke these words to illustrate
We'll get our reward if we just wait,
We'll be gathered up when His net is cast.
The last will be first and the first will be last

Partying On.

"Let me go dear father, I don't want to stay,
I'm young only once father, I want to live life and play.
Give me my share dear father, my inheritance please,
And let me go partying on".

With heart overburdened, by sorrow and woe,
The father watched as his son, on his journey he did go.
He gave him his share of all that he had
Allowing him to go partying on.

So off to the bright lights with joy in his heart,
The son searched for the place where his party would start.
He soon found some friends who joined him as he found
The place to go partying on.

Time passed and wine flowed, and all were at peace.
The son dreamed his new life, and times would not cease
He had not a care for what tomorrow might bring,
Wanting to be partying on.

But one day in the inn with his hand in his purse,
No money was found and the son he did curse,
He had not a coin to pay for his fayre,
To let him keep partying on.

He looked right then looked left and swung on his chair.
Looked hard for his friends, who no longer where there.
He was there all alone, no one else could be found
To help him go partying on.

Finding a job was the next task he had,
His mood was morose, his demeanour was sad,
He thought "what a fool I was to spend my whole life
Longing to be partying on".

As hunger and thirst ravaged his body and mind,
He thought of his home, and the peace he would find,
If only his father would forgive his desire,
To spend his life partying on.

He decided he would swallow his pride and return,
For the warmth and the comfort of home, he did yearn.
He would ask for forgiveness, for wasting his life
He'd spent always partying on.

As he approached from a distance, his father did see,
And said "My dearest lost son is returning to me.
The fatted calf, go and kill, make merry today,
My son has stopped partying on".

Coming back from his work cultivating the ground,
The eldest son heard celebrations and sound.
Discovered they were held for his brothers' return,
Who no longer was partying on.

"Father what does this mean, I have done you no wrong,
I've been faithful and loyal to you, all the day long,
Not once did you thank me for staying around,
As my brother went partying on".

"My son don't be angry, all I have left is yours,
Your brothers returned, see he's waiting indoors.
He's so sorry he left us, and wasted his life,
Spending time always partying on.

For so many years I had thought that my son had died,
I shed many tears, every night, as I cried,
Just longing for him to return to the fold,
And ceasing his partying on.

Your brother once thought dead, is now much alive
He's returned to us, how can we him our love deprive?
He's found here at home is the best place to be,
Not out there ever partying on".

The Needle's Eye

A rich man came to Jesus as he walked around one day,
He approached him, he was nervous, a question to convey.
He walked right up to Jesus, who had disciples all around,
The man acknowledged Jesus' goodness, as he stood there on the ground.

It's easier for a camel to go through a needles tiny eye,
Than for the wealthy to enter heaven, even though they try.

"Teacher please instruct me, on the way I can be saved.
I live a life that's blameless, you can say I'm well behaved,
I want to go to heaven, I want to live there with the blessed,
Teach me oh blessed saviour, how I can have eternal rest".

It's easier for a camel to go through a needles tiny eye,
Than for the wealthy to enter heaven, even though they try.

Then Jesus said "Be faithful and do all that Gods commands,
If you keep the prophets' teachings, you'll be safe inside Gods hands".
"I do these now I know it, I've kept them all from birth,
These teachings they of value, I appreciate their worth".

It's easier for a camel to go through a needles tiny eye,
Than for the wealthy to enter heaven, even though they try.

"It's good that you are faithful and you recognise Gods plan,
But there's one more thing to combat, are you really sure you can?
You're a man with many treasures, sell them all and follow me,
Give the money to the needy, and their happiness you will see".

It's easier for a camel to go through a needles tiny eye,
Than for the wealthy to enter heaven, even though they try.

The man closed his eyes and turning, walked away heart full of woe,
He had so many riches and he knew he loved them so.
He couldn't lose his comfort, his position in social life,
The words that Jesus uttered, they had cut him like a knife.

It's easier for a camel to go through a needles tiny eye,
Than for the wealthy to enter heaven, even though they try.

It's true the love of money, will a multitude destroy,
For many it is their passion, and all its comforts they enjoy.
This passion is destructive, with consequences lethal,
For they'll be cast into torment, not in heaven all calm and peaceful.

It's easier for a camel to go through a needles tiny eye,
Than for the wealthy to enter heaven, even though they try.

The Old Man

The old man lay in torment, as he waited for the news
Worrying if he'd be successful, in his medical reviews.
He was not scared of dying, he believed he would be saved.
"There's never walked on earth a man, so impeccably behaved.

I've lived a life of service, and cared for my weaker fellow man,
If anyone can be applauded, surely, I am one of those who can.
And yes, I have my riches, locked away from thieving hands,
I've gathered many treasures from many far off, foreign lands.

I've made sure they're all looked after, in a dark and secure vault,
And if other people struggle, well then, surely that's not my fault.
The talents with which God's blessed me, I've used the best that I know how,
Although I've never worked in factories, or even had a field to plough.

My skills have been in business closing many a lucrative deal,
I admit to looking over shoulders, to see what secrets I could steal.
I have cut many numerous corners, and some minuscule truths I've bent,
But I'm sure I've been forgiven, for each time, I did repent.

Looking back, I've helped such people, who by the world had been ignored,
By wishing them wealth and happiness, oh how my satisfaction soared.
I've never failed in my standing, imparting advice when er' I can,
I've never discriminated against a woman, or against a man.

There's been times I've even suffered, when trying to ease a person's pain,
Making great noises of derision, if they returned and asked again.
They thought they were the only ones, who ever needed aid,
And their faces when I contributed they looked, well ever so dismayed.

Did they think that I would empty my bank vault to make them well?
It was not my fault that they all suffered, not my fault their debts did swell.
They all believed I gave a pittance, really thinking I was tight,
I'm sure there is a story in the bible about a widow's mite?

My contribution may be tiny, and to some people may seem small,
But I need a financial cushion in case the markets reverse and fall.
Now just where is my doctor, when will he return and bring me news,
Regarding my condition, will I with happiness infuse?

Oh, here he is the door has opened, and somebody's coming in,
But it doesn't look like he's my doctor, his face is masked and hid within.
He's walking like a shadow, softly gliding across the floor,
Now come to think of it, on entering, he passed right through the door.

The door it did not open, but that is what I first thought,
So who is this dark strange being, what sort of news has he now brought?
He's saying my life is ending, on this plane I've thought as home,
And the behaviour of my existence to myself, now will be shown.

He's taking me to moments I've been asked to offer aid,
And help the ones less able to provide for, their table laid.
He takes me to a place with many people there, inside,
I try to pull away, I'm frightened, but there is nowhere I can hide.

I see me sitting at a table in my fine array of clothes,
I really look quite dashing, with my much superior pose.
People are standing looking hungry, their plates are empty, with no food,
They're watching while I'm eating; well now that's just very rude.

My plates are filled with plenty, food is spilling on the floor,
I don't share with all the watchers, I'm sure they'd only ask for more.
I tell them they can have some, when my stomach is full inside,
And when I look across toward them, each one of them has died.

Looking closely at the people lying stiff upon the floor,
Recognising many faces, some I'm sure I've seen before.
These are people who approached me, asking for a little aid,
I just turned my back upon them, leaving each of them dismayed.

I'm then taken to the homes, with many children cold and bare,
Crying loudly for their father, but their father wasn't there.
Mothers sitting in the corners, tears are streaming from their eyes,
I didn't know they were that desperate, I really didn't realise.

I thought they all were lazy, wanting wealth from me to scrounge,
Wanting me to give them money, and then just go back home to lounge.
My eyes with tears were filling, sobs and sorrow fill my heart,
I really want to help them but, I don't know where to start.

Is it too late I ask this stranger, is it too late to make amends?
I look to him for an answer, but his arm forward he extends,
He's pointing to the future, but there is nothing I can see,
Then a light out from the distance is coming closer, now, to me.

A voice comes out of nowhere, "You will get a second chance,
To repair your eternal standing, it's up to you to change your stance
About your desire for earthly riches, and the wealth you do pursue.
If you want to help those people, my friend it's really up to you".

I awoke, my eyes they opened, was all I saw a dream?
There was no body in my room now, I asked myself, what did it mean?
I have money that's a given, but I've no friends no family,
In my home there's just one person, and that one person is just me.

I thought I was self-sufficient, never needing other folk,
But when I look more closely, my life is really one big joke.
Sure, I'm rich, I lack for nothing, what I want I go and get,
I should be happy with all my money, I should be satisfied, but yet,

There must be other values that I can find, while on this earth
Better values that have been with me since, the moment of my birth.
I've lusted after money, wealth has been my one desire,
But it's no good me being wealthy if I burn in Hades fire.

I will make some alterations, I won't waste my final chance,
There are many ways I know how other lives, I can enhance".
Then the doctor makes an entrance, walking slowly to the bed,
His eyes are full of feeling and he slowly shakes his head,

It seems you are getting better, it is to us, a big surprise
It's a wonderful improvement", then a smile came to his eyes.
"Whatever happened take advantage, that's my best advice to you.
If an opportunity beckons, try your best to see it through.

In the bible Jesus tells us if earth's treasures we do crave,
We will miss the gospel message which is, that Jesus came to save.
He came to save us all from evil, came to save us from the fire
That awaits the lost in Hades, to save our souls is his desire.

He offers us so many treasures, that rust and rot cannot consume,
Treasures waiting in his mansion, and for each one of us a room.
If we chase only earthly pleasures, and the word of him deride,
We will have a rude awakening when our human flesh has died,

But if we hunger for the goodness of the love, our Lord does give,
We'll be welcomed into heaven, and in paradise we'll live.
Now the old man has satisfaction, putting smiles on every face,
As he shares with them Gods blessings, telling them about God's grace.

No longer is he lonely, no heavy heart filled with despair,
He knows if he ever needs him, his saviour will be there.
The message Jesus gives us about the riches of the world,
Is how they lose their value when eternity's unfurled.

The treasure that he offers, it won't devalue, rust or fade,
And through his holy gospel, this treasure is conveyed.
He offers it to all men, showing no partiality,
And if we lovingly pursue it, this treasure makes us free.

Strangled by Thorns

The seed was sown it fell upon
The rocky solid ground,
The wind it came and blew the seeds,
They were scattered all around.

Birds flew over, picked up some
And took them to their nest.
They took all those that they could find,
The sun shone down and burnt the rest.

The seed was sown, it found a home
In shallow fertile ground,
It took its root, began to grow
But no strength was to be found.

Those shallow roots, they had no chance
They withered, grew so weak.
Had failed attempts to find some food,
With great effort they did seek.

The seed was sown, it found a home
Amongst the thorns and weeds,
But as it grew began to bloom
It found thorns, growth impedes.

No matter how the seed did try,
The thorns choked any growth,
And soon the seed began to die,
Lost in the undergrowth.

The seed was sown, it found a home
In soil so rich, and pure,
It grew so strong and able,
Life's pressures, to endure.

The seed grew high and brought much fruit
Which the farmer did admire,
While he cleared up all the wasted seeds
Throwing them into the fire.

The seed which thrown, it is God's word,
The soil it is our life.
The quality of the soil we have,
Affects our afterlife.

Will we be soil so full of weeds?
Or thorns, or maybe both.
Or will our soil bring forth much fruit,
And escape the undergrowth.

In an Upper Room.

Gathered in an upper room,
Away from prying eyes,
A group of men were meeting,
Wondering what in life before them, lies?
Gathered in an upper room,
They talked about the tomb,
And how they'd laid their master there,
How they let their grief consume.

Gathered in an upper room,
They discussed what Jesus said,
About how he would be crucified
And then rise up from the dead.
Gathered in an upper room,
They talked about the days,
When Jesus first appeared to them,
Telling them they were not dazed.

Gathered in an upper room,
They talked about the things he'd shared,
Of how he ate and drank with them,
No part of him impaired.
Gathered in an upper room,
They discussed watching him go.
They all wished he was there with them,
They truly missed him so.

Gathered in an upper room,
They wondered what they'd do,
Now Jesus had returned to heaven,
And they were only few.
Gathered in an upper room,
Their hearts were full of fear,
They road that lay before them all,
Its' direction was not clear.

Gathered in an upper room,
They heard a rushing sound,
It was the helper promised them,
They felt its power all around.
Gathered in an upper room,
Apostles now were changed,
From not knowing where the path would lead,
Their life's plan, was rearranged.

Leaving now that upper room,
Into the streets they went,
To preach about the saviour who
From heaven, was for them sent.
No longer in that upper room,
They preached throughout the world
And Gods salvation plan for man,
Systematically was unfurled.

No longer in that upper room,
No need to hide away,
They preached that Jesus said he would
Return to judge, one day.
They went into that upper room,
Unsure of what to do.
Now Christ's' word's preached to everyone,
It began with just a few.

Something's Happening Here

Something's happening here,
And what it is, to me is not clear,
There was a man sitting near on a chair,
But when I looked, the man was not there.
Where has my friend gone,
We once were two and now we are one.

I hear of things going on,
People are here but the next minute gone.
A man and wife, they were lying in bed,
He touched the place where once lay her head.
Where has his wife gone,
Once they were two and now they are one.

People they cry in the street,
Sharing tales with each one they meet,
Two people walking this day up a hill,
One disappeared and ones left standing still.
Where has his friend gone,
Once they were two and now they are one.

Now what's that sound that I hear,
A golden light now all things become clear,
The Son of Man in His glory so bright,
Gathering those who have finished the fight.
I know where they have gone,
They've been welcomed by the blessed one.

Oh why did I not believe,
Now it's too late the truth to retrieve,
Was offered hope, but I turned it down,
Forfeiting chance, for a golden crown.
I now will be cast away,
My punishment on judgement day.

I awake I'm still tucked up in bed,
Visions of judgement they whirl 'round my head.
I now have things that I need to change,
My chosen path, I must rearrange.
I know now what I must do,
If I want to join the blessed few.

I must believe in Him who died,
Our risen Lord who was crucified,
He gave His life to allow you and me,
From dreadful sin, to be set free.
He is the life the truth and way,
And will welcome us on judgement day.

Talking to the Dead Men.

People listened to the speaker
As he spoke about great things.
Proclaiming all the bounteous gifts
Coming from the king of kings.
About the life in heaven
Offered to each and every man
Of peace and of salvation
By following Gods' plan.
But he was talking to the dead men,
Happy with their lot
Convinced that they were going to Heaven,
Sadly, they were not.

"Another crank is speaking,
Wanting to change the world.
There always has been someone
Since time was itself unfurled".
"He looks a pleasant fellow,
Let's give the lad a chance".
But some of those that gathered,
Tried to weave a merry dance.
But he was talking to the dead men,
Happy with their lot
Convinced that they were going to Heaven,
Sadly, they were not.

"What makes you think you're better?
What makes you think you're right?
We like the life we have been living,
Why the good fight should we fight?
You know this Saviour Jesus,
You say he has all power,
But he couldn't turn the tables
In His crucifixion hour".
But he was talking to the dead men,
Happy with their lot
Convinced that they were going to Heaven,
Sadly, they were not.

"Don't you understand it,
Our Saviour, chose to die,
To prepare for us a mansion
In His home beyond the sky.
His power it is unceasing,
His love it will prevail,
And all of Satan's' armies
In spiritual wars will fail".
But he was talking to the dead men,
Happy with their lot
Convinced that they were going to Heaven,
Sadly, they were not.

"Off you go then preacher,
your words we do not need.
They won't clothe our aching backs
And our children they won't feed.
We don't need your Saviour,
We will make it on our own.
Get lost, we have no interest
In what you have to say".
But he was talking to the dead men,
Happy with their lot
Convinced that they were going to Heaven,
Sadly, they were not.

The preacher stood in silence,
Tears trickled from his eye,
He thought that they'd love Jesus,
But found He was despised.
They people all knew better,
Or that's what they did think.
They were marching towards destruction,
All hovering on the brink.
But he was talking to the dead men,
Happy with their lot
Convinced that they were going to Heaven,
Sadly, they were not.

Sadly, with fallen shoulders,
The preacher turned to go
Feeling sorry for the people
Because he loved them so.
From the pit he tried to save them,
But they all ignored what he did say.
Believe their own devices
Will save them on judgment day.
Yes, he was talking to the dead men,
Happy with their lot
Convinced that they were going to Heaven,
Sadly, they were not.

If you're standing with the dead men,
Its time to take a look
And see what God can offer you,
It's all inside His book.
Don't be fooled by all the doubters
Don't follow their evil way,
Remember Christ will judge all men
When He returns One Day.
Then He will send the dead men
Into darkness with all their sin,
Where men will weep and gnash their teeth
While the living abide with Him.

QUESTIONS & DOUBT

Where Did Your Faith Go?

Where did your faith go,
When the storm clouds first appeared?
Where did your faith go,
When the thunderclaps you heard?
As you sailed the seas of life,
And waves buffered to and fro,
Being filled with stress and strife,
Tell me, where did your faith go?

Once you were steadfast
Trusting in God's precious word,
What happened to bring steadfast,
Believing in Him who cared?
When walking on the pathway,
And the storm winds roar and blow,
Why did you lose your trust in Jesus?
Tell me, where did your faith go?

Did words you heard once spoken,
Evolve in an empty heart?
Did your ringing clanging noises,
Bring forth deceit, right from the start?
Speaking always with a forked tongue
Spouting lies led from below,
When asked to speak up for Jesus,
Tell me, where did your faith go?

Professing profound belief,
In truth and spiritual birth,
Declaring your love and faith
In Him, who gave us, His worth,
When the crowd with you disagreed
Telling you that it is not so,
When it was your time to confess Him,
Tell me, where did your faith go?

Tell me, how far can you go
Before you run out of lies?
When your life is called to account,
Is it then you will realise,
Have you been wasting precious moments,
Have you been putting on a show?
What will you say when Jesus asks you,
"Tell me, where did your faith go?"

Hold His Hand

A drowning man forlorn and lost,
Is floating to and fro,
He has no indication of
Where next his soul will go.
He gasps for air and splutters,
As salt water he inhales.
And makes its way into his lungs,
Engulfing his entrails.

He thinks he will be joining those
Over time in seas have drowned.
Until he hears a noise behind,
And turns his head around.
A craft so small is sailing there,
He knows now, he'll reach dry land,
The first thing he now has to do,
Is offer up his hand.

Out goes his hand he reaches for
His saviour in the craft.
And then he's hoisted up on board,
Stored safely in the aft.
The man said he'd been calling him
Since first he saw his head,
And if he refused to stretch his hand,
He's sure he would be dead.

A climber on a mountain high,
Surrounded by his peers.
Was walking with his head aloft,
No thought of any fears.
Then all at once, no warning given,
His feet began to slide
There was no place that he could run,
For him no place to hide.

How quickly did he lose his grip,
And panic fill his heart?
He tried to hold tight on the rope,
But descending he did start.
He fell down deep into a hole,
That suddenly did appear,
A rope was sent to where he lay,
And "Grab hold" our friend did hear.

Then he reached out for the rope,
Wrapped safely 'round his wrist.
He then was slowly lifted out
Into the freezing mist.
Pats on his back and hugs from all,
Grateful words filled up his head,
Knowing if he hadn't grabbed the rope,
He's sure he would be dead.

Over many years of living,
Men have travelled their own way.
They all thought they had the answer,
Ignoring what the Christ did say.
Immersed in pride and self-loving,
Thinking they were life's first prize.
Ignorant of what was waiting,
When they finally closed their eyes.

All souls who wander about earth
And sail the sea of life,
Through many stormy waters,
Are attacked, by fears and strife.
They all need a guide to lead them
All into the promised land.
And your captain, He is waiting,
For you, to hold His hand.

Take Christ's hand, and hold on tightly,
He is reaching out to you.
Let him take control and lead you,
Into your home, beyond the blue.
He is our loving friend, so faithful,
He frees our sinful soul from dread.
And know if we release his hand,
Without Him we are dead.

I Have No Time for Jesus.

"I have no time for Jesus" the boy said to the man,
"I know just what I want from life, I'll do the best I can,
My aim is lots of money, enough to see me through
The problems that will arise each day, I'm happier than you".

"But when the market stutters, and the interest rates they rise,
When your pockets they are empty and your heart is full of sighs,
Will you then sleep easy with no worries on your mind,
Or will the tranquillisers help you to unwind.

Our Lord recalled a story of a man once rich who died,
And standing there in judgement turned to Abraham and cried,
"In my family I have brothers I must be allowed to warn
So they won't be found in torment on their resurrection morn".

"But what about the prophets?" to him the Lord decreed,
"If to hand they have their answers, what more warning could they need?"
So standing there in torment, the man adrift from life,
Knew he could not get a warning to his brothers or his wife.

We have the Lords instructions on how not to give much room
To the building up of treasures where moths and rust consume.
If we want to live forever and eternal glory share,
Our aim must be the crown of life eternally to wear".

The boy who sat in silence sighed and slowly turned his head
"If I build up wealth in life I'll only lose it when I'm dead,
You've filled my head with thoughts and words about which road to take,
Do I seek the wealth of heaven, or eternal life forsake?"

Hold Out Your Hand

Hold your hand out toward me, please Jesus,
My steps are unsteady and weak,
I'm a work incomplete but in progress,
Grant me the guidance and love that I seek.

When the seas get so rough and wind billows,
Forcing me far away from the land,
When I need you to help in my turmoil,
Dear Saviour, please hold out your hand.

When my steps get so weak and I'm burdened,
And I cannot be stable and stand,
When I need your support for my guidance.
Dear Saviour, please hold out your hand.

I fail many times blessed Saviour,
But I know that you do understand.
When I'm needing a guide through temptation,
Dear Saviour, please hold out your hand.

I know that your road leads to heaven,
In the beginning you had it all planned,
Even though I am weak and I falter,
Dear Saviour, please hold out your hand.

I know you are always there with me.
And all creation is at your command.
I know I can be sure of your promise,
Dear Saviour, please hold out your hand.

Hold your hand out toward me, please Jesus,
My steps are unsteady and weak,
I'm a work incomplete but in progress,
Grant me the guidance and love that I seek.

On Which Side Will You Be?

It's a spirit deep inside us, no one can hear, no one can see.
It never dies it is eternal, but to live, where will that be?
Will it live in heaven and glory, resting with all the saints gone by,
Or be cast into eternal torment, inside a darkness, with no sky?

On that day of promised judgment, when we hear his trumpet sound,
When Jesus returns in glory, raising souls deep from the ground.
And from watery depths come others, who all lost their lives at sea,
When that judgment day comes pilgrim, on which side will you be?

From our moment of conception, when our seed of life was formed,
And we grew inside our mothers, in a womb, so safe and warmed.
Then came the day of our arrival, into this sinful world outside,
When there was such joy and laughter, that very moment we first cried.

On that day of promised judgment, when we hear his trumpet sound,
When Jesus returns in glory, raising souls deep from the ground.
And from watery depths come others, who all lost their lives at sea,
When that judgment day comes pilgrim, on which side will you be?

Growing up so many lessons, we had to learn to make our way.
In a world with contradictions, swarming around us every day.
We had parents there to guide us, teaching us the wrong from right,
But much teaching was distorted, which could lead to endless night.

On that day of promised judgment, when we hear his trumpet sound,
When Jesus returns in glory, raising souls deep from the ground.
And from watery depths come others, who all lost their lives at sea,
When that judgment day comes pilgrim, on which side will you be?

So much to learn and to decipher, lots of opinions fill our heads,
Some are holding very tenuously, to actual truth by fragile threads.
But our search brings many questions about how it came to be,
Man thought he knew the answer, but blinded people cannot see.

On that day of promised judgment, when we hear his trumpet sound,
When Jesus returns in glory, raising souls deep from the ground.
And from watery depths come others, who all lost their lives at sea,
When that judgment day comes pilgrim, on which side will you be?

Why do men put so much value in striving to be rich,
Only to find they're left in sorrow, when the sea of life does pitch?
When they find that they are empty, after their treasures have all gone,
And find they have no sure foundation, their loss continues on.

On that day of promised judgment, when we hear his trumpet sound,
When Jesus returns in glory, raising souls deep from the ground.
And from watery depths come others, who all lost their lives at sea,
When that judgment day comes pilgrim, on which side will you be?

Throughout ages many leaders, deceived by selfishness and pride,
Concerned more with their appearance, while hiding ugliness inside
Made acclamation from their public, the culmination of their goal,
No concern of their salvation, or the destination of their soul.

On that day of promised judgment, when we hear his trumpet sound,
When Jesus returns in glory, raising souls deep from the ground.
And from watery depths come others, who all lost their lives at sea,
When that judgment day comes pilgrim, on which side will you be?

The written words of scripture, blessed by the spirit of the Lord,
Taught all those that worshipped Jesus, were to speak with one accord.
They had instructions and much guidance, all they needed to be saved,
No changes were required, to how the message was relayed.

On that day of promised judgment, when we hear his trumpet sound,
When Jesus returns in glory, raising souls deep from the ground.
And from watery depths come others, who all lost their lives at sea,
When that judgment day comes pilgrim, on which side will you be?

Mankind immersed in ego, believed the message was all wrong.
Saying it was full of twisted meanings, it's deceived us all along.
They ignored all Gods instructions, of where unfaithful changes led,
Ignored the pathway up to heaven, taking the path to hell instead.

On that day of promised judgment, when we hear his trumpet sound,
When Jesus returns in glory, raising souls deep from the ground.
And from watery depths come others, who all lost their lives at sea,
When that judgment day comes pilgrim, on which side will you be?

Our Heavenly Father gave a promise, in many ages now gone by,
That the saved will all be gathered into their mansion, in the sky.
A crown of life will then be given to each soul, who ran the race.
And will find comfort in his bosom, full of love and full of grace.

On that day of promised judgment, when we hear his trumpet sound,
When Jesus returns in glory, raising souls deep from the ground.
And from watery depths come others, who all lost their lives at sea,
When that judgment day comes pilgrim, on which side will you be?

But those who rejected Jesus, and defied our gracious Lord,
Will be thrown into outer darkness, cast adrift from Jesus' chord.
In that place, they will be punished, as the word does clearly say.
Being tormented there forever, no time for rest, no time for play.

On that day of promised judgment, when we hear his trumpet sound,
When Jesus returns in glory, raising souls deep from the ground.
And from watery depths come others, who all lost their lives at sea,
When that judgment day comes pilgrim, on which side will you be?

We are given many warnings as we read the sacred word,
Which tells of God's forgiveness, and how much our Father cared,
How he sent his son to suffer death, bound high on Calvary's tree.
Where he suffered pain and anguish, for our sins us to set us free.

On that day of promised judgment, when we hear his trumpet sound,
When Jesus returns in glory, raising souls deep from the ground.
And from watery depths come others, who all lost their lives at sea,
When that judgment day comes pilgrim, on which side will you be?

On that day of promised judgment, when all the dead from Earth will rise,
And they stand before their maker, as they meet him in the skies,
Each ones' book of life will open, telling of everything they've done,
Whether they've rejected Jesus, or obeyed Gods only son.

On that day of promised judgment, when we hear his trumpet sound,
When Jesus returns in glory, raising souls deep from the ground.
And from watery depths come others, who all lost their lives at sea,
When that judgment day comes pilgrim, on which side will you be?

What Will He Do?

Intentions they mean nothing,
If you're walking the wrong road.
Torn between both good and evil,
Struggling with guilt that's being bestowed.
It really isn't easy
Two minds in one man's brain.
One attempting to take the Lords way,
Then being rebounded back again.
To live a life so abstract
With everything surreal,
Unable to be focused,
Confusion is all you feel.
But how long do you struggle,
Before your troubled mind implodes,
With thoughts of guilt and longing,
Your tortured soul corrodes?
Each day the war is raging,
Each day many tears are shed.
There is no truce to offer
Both sides fighting in your head.
It's like living in a theatre,
Watching actors in a play.
Will the hero choose the right road,
Or will he stumble the wrong way?
Will he make the right decision,
Following the path of light?
Will he close his mind to reason,
And live in a world of endless night?
The weariness of turmoil
Fills him with tension, stress and more.
Will he be cast out into darkness,
Or bathe in light through heaven's door?

The Trader

The trader sat, made many plans,
How he could go and sell
All of his goods, home and abroad
Wherever his shadow fell.
He spent much time perfecting ways
His bank balance to greatly swell.
He'd be so important the people around,
His station they could tell.

Oh, the folly of the man
Not giving any thought,
To whether God had for him a plan
No guidance had he sought.

For many days he bought his stock,
His very last coin, he spent
To all his traders far and wide,
His adverts he had sent.
He worked so hard, his body tired
But his efforts would not relent.
And although he spent much time in sin,
He made no time to repent.

Oh, the folly of the man
Not giving any thought,
To whether God had for him a plan
No guidance had he sought.

When final plans where all in place,
The time came to rest his head.
And though he thought of saying prayers,
He checked through his books instead.
No time to thank God for his life,
No interest in what Jesus said.
Any thought to change would come too late,
For by the morning, he was dead.

Oh, the folly of the man
Not giving any thought,
To whether God had for him a plan
No guidance had he sought.

Around his corpse lay all his books,
Amongst the plans he'd made.
And people who relied on him,
All of them he had betrayed.
He chased the gold and pearls of earth,
So his power could be displayed.
He scorned the crown God offered him,
And the treasure that will never fade.

Oh, the folly of the man
Not giving any thought,
To whether God had for him a plan
No guidance had he sought.

Oh, foolish man for putting faith,
In things that fade and rust,
For yearning riches from the earth,
Which will all in time be dust.
He spurned the chance to change his ways,
To end his worldly pleasures lust,
And yearn for riches there above
For those who in their God trust.

The foolish man chose Satan's way
And closed his mind to Him,
Who sacrificed his son for us,
And cleansed us from our sin.

Questions

What will you do when you hear the trumpet sound?
What will you do, when your feet lift off the ground?
What will you do, when the Lord again appears?
Will your heart fill up with joy, or be full of endless fears?

What will you do when the light fills up the sky?
What will you do, when your memories pass you by?
What will you do, when at last you realise,
The gospel spoke Gods truth wherein salvation lies?

What will you do when you stand before the Lord?
What will you feel, when you finally meet God's Word?
What will you do, when the Lord calls out your name
Will you finally believe, it was for you He came?

What will you think, of the chances that you spurned?
What thoughts now, of the lessons never learned?
What will you think, of times you chose the devils road?
How wearied now you've struggled daily with sins load?

What will you feel, when you're cast into the fire?
How fierce the pain, when the flames keep climbing higher?
What will it be, that torments you the most?
Will it be your rejection of the blessed Holy Ghost?

What waits for you on judgement day my friend?
Will despair and pain be waiting, at your life's journey's end?
Is there for you an eternal flaming fire,
Where unquenched coals are heaped on the ever-burning pyre?

What can you do to change the way you live
And break the chains that are holding you captive?
How can you turn from the road that leads to pain
And take the road that leads to eternal gain?

What can you do to enter in Gods bliss?
Are you concerned, Heaven's chances you will miss?
Are you aware your life span may be short?
Do you believe now with Christ's blood you were bought?

Will you reject all the good the Lord has done?
Will you ignore God has sent His only son?
Will you accept He wants to save us all?
Will you now give all your attention to His call?

Who Sends the Voice?

Where do they come from?
Who sends them our way?
Some pass quickly moving,
Some make home and stay.
Some bring help with problems,
Which cause us to stress.
Some churn up bad feelings
Increasing duress.
Some go on repeating
Advice or a doubt.
When these find an anchor,
They're hard to push out.
They cling like a snail
On a glass or on a wall.
Sometimes we can't shake them
Or ignore them at all.
We don't know who sends them,
They just seem to appear.
Some come like a whisper
Not easy to hear.
Some come like a klaxon
Its noise is so loud
It drowns out the volume
When you're in a crowd.
So where do they come from
And to where do they go?
Are words that invade us,
From above or below?
They say it's our conscience
Guiding us on our way,
If they're trying to help us,
Why don't they just say?
At times when we're thinking
About the meaning of life,
When our thoughts are of peace,
They can revert back to strife.
We cannot control them,
Or censor our thought.
Once they enter the process,
We're left with all they have brought.
All the words that we're hearing
We have heard or we've read,
We just opened the door,
And let them inside our head.
We can take back control
Influencing our mind,
Ensure what we're seeking,
Is what we will find.
If we censor our reading,
And watch all we imbibe,
We can fill up our minds
Letting goodness inside.
We can stop all the bad words
From polluting our brain,
Substituting their evil
With good words, again.

If we fill up with rubbish,
That's all we will think.
And in a sea full of evil,
We will gradually sink.
But the words of the good book
If we spend time to learn,
Absorbing God's teachings
Then Satan we'll spurn.
We'll build our defences
When the storm clouds do swell,
Knowing if we spurn Jesus,
Our road leads to hell.
But by making an effort
And deciding our path,
We'll be saved at the calling
And escape from God's wrath.
It's our mind that we carry
Around in our head,
We can free it from evil,
Fill it with goodness instead.
Our eyes and our ears,
Are doors leading within,
And it's still not too late
Our life's path to begin.

Will Man Change?

All the oil ran out, all the gold ran out,
All the water ran out, all the food ran out,
All the diamonds ran out, all the pearls ran out,
All the jewels ran out, all their hope ran out,
But Gods love continues on.

The people ran from place to place
To find somewhere to hide,
They carried treasures on their backs,
No horses left to ride.
No cars had they to drive around,
No petrol for their tanks,
No one to guide them through the day,
Bringing order to the ranks.
All aircraft rested on the ground,
Grass growing 'round their wheels.
Ships in the harbour, which now had rust
Replacing paint, that peels.
Transport links ground to a halt,
No trains out riding rails,
No breaking records with their speed,
Now beaten by the snails.
And so the people rush around,
No order in their mind.
No place to rest their weary head,
There's sanctuary to find.
A bursting rabble making noise,
Social conscience gone,
Afraid to offer any help,
Afraid of everyone.
No offer of a helping hand
To infants who are lost.
The people turn their backs on them
They're just collateral cost.
The screaming, shouting yelling throng,
Had put their faith in all
The things of earth, which rust and fade,
And ignored the saviours call.
No great desire to give to Him
Who reigns in heaven above,
A moment of their precious time
To think about His love.
And all the wealth that's waiting for
The faithful and the blessed,
Who have a home awaiting them,
In Gods eternal rest.
Continuing they run around,
Minds filled with deadly fear,
They're not as rich as they once were
And their predicament is clear.
Still holding on to what they had
Not believing all is lost,
Their situation they can't grasp,
And it's come at such a cost.
The worldly wealth that they've accrued
Over many, many years.

Has disappeared before their eyes,
Which now are filled with tears.
Where now to go for sanctuary
Safe from the baying throng,
Which new place will be their home,
To where, will they belong?
Oh how did all things come to this
They felt safe and secure,
How could their lifestyle change so much,
Their wealth, their peace, and more?
They had respect from everyone, who
They encountered on their way.
And invites to best films and balls,
Came flooding in each day.
They gave no consideration,
Of how shallow they had been,
How foolishly they'd spent their days,
Rejecting wealth, unseen.
Engrossed in chasing treasures which,
They believed would satisfy,
But their greed grew ravenous
As each day went passing by.
And now they run from place to place,
There's nowhere they can hide.
And a seeping desperation,
Like a cancer grows inside.
Wrapped in disillusionment
They were the tainted upper class,
They thought they'd always have it all,
But things have changed, alas.
The worldly wealth, they once did have,
Has all but disappeared,
And now their situation is
Much worse, than they had feared.
If only they had realised,
And given any thought,
Or credence to the very one,
With whose blood they all were bought.
Eyes blinded by their worldly lust,
They with loathing did reject,
The loving word that's free to all,
Only wealth did they respect.
The friends they could rely upon
Are now lost amongst the mass
Of heaving individuals,
There's no time now for class.
Only one class now existing,
All status is the same,
Despair is rife in everyone,
Who thought life was a game.
Each class had different values,
Although existing side by side,
But the same fate, it waits for all,
As they search, where they can hide.
No time to care for anyone,
Survival is the key.
Most rejecting constantly the truth,
Sent to all, to set them free.

How foolish now their values,
What they cling to is worth nought.
How priceless now the blood once shed,
With which their lives where bought.
The priceless gift, worth more than all
The treasures of the world.
Have been there for the taking,
Since Gods' promise was unfurled.
Confusion in their troubled minds,
Tears streaming down each face.
Oh how things would be different,
If they accepted Gods' good grace.
Maybe when they find some rest,
With family close at hand,
Will they re-evaluate,
Will they come to understand?
Will they stop and think about
The wealth, that they once had,
The loss of which brought deep distress,
The loss which made them sad?
Will they search beyond this sphere,
Where nothing ever lasts?
Turning their thoughts to heaven above,
Where their expectations are surpassed?
How long will people close their eyes,
Bringing darkness to their soul?
Will they take time to give a thought
To the love, that makes men whole?
Or continue down the path that leads
Away from endless night,
And travel to where Jesus is,
Guided by their saviours' light?
Their saviour who is always there,
Just waiting for their call,
With open arms, and helping hands,
Supporting those that trip and fall.
The promise God gave so long ago
Was one day he would send
His son, who would take human form,
Preaching love that has no end.
He only asks we put our trust
In Him, our heavenly guide.
Believing, as we walk each day,
He is there right by our side.
But there are those who turn their backs,
And ignore the saviours call.
Putting trust in him who calls the lost,
And enlist in Satan's fall.
Such vanity for personal gain,
Such shallow wants, and needs,
Bring feelings wrapped in deep despair,
Increasing, as their wealth recedes.
Worldly people invest their faith
In material, transient things,
Refusing to embrace Gods love,
And all the peace it brings.

They let the evil one confuse
Their hearts, and lead them on,
Down to the place where they are lost
And where all hope is gone.
He fills their minds with evil thoughts,
Offering worldly wealth to all,
Who bend and give heed to his words,
Disbelieve they're heading for a fall.
He leads astray each deceived heart,
To their own eternal doom,
Where death and pain awaits for those
Who willingly give him room.
But there are those, amongst the crowd
Who have hope beyond this earth,
Putting their faith in God above,
Who has loved them from their birth.
They have put their faith in riches, which
Will neither fade nor rust,
And seek Him on his heavenly throne,
Whose judgement they can trust.
This God of theirs holds out His hands,
And gathers safely in,
All those believing in His son,
Who has saved them from their sin.
The others who ignore Gods word,
Have lessons much to learn,
About the riches they can have,
If they just to him turn.
Salvation is what Jesus taught,
To all who truly do believe,
And repent of all their sinful ways,
Their dreadful burden he'll relieve.
There is no charge, it's all been paid,
We don't have to foot the cost.
God offers wealth that will not fade,
And pardon, for the lost.
Still people all career around,
Cling to treasures of the past.
They have confidence, but it will fade,
They have hope that will not last.
Memories of their lives now gone,
Invade their troubled mind,
They search each place for sanctuary,
But its peace, they cannot find.
Oh foolish men, can you not see,
How you have wasted so much time,
Rejecting God who offers life,
And his peace, which is sublime?
Surrounded by a milling crowd,
Devastated by their loss,
Determined to ignore the call
Made by Jesus, from his cross.
Now is time to give a thought
To Him who does not change,
And take each opportunity,
All your lives to rearrange.

The life they'd known is past and gone,
Mankind must start again.
So much to learn, so much they've lost,
Old skills they must regain.

A slower pace of life exists
Now there's time to reassess,
The shallowness of values, which,
Left their lives in such a mess.
Will they change? Nobody knows,
Surely, they're not that blind to see,
If they put their faith in things that rust,
They'll be lost for eternity.

All the oil ran out, all the gold ran out,
All the water ran out, all the food ran out,
All the diamonds ran out, all the pearls ran out,
All the jewels ran out, all their hope ran out,
But Gods love continues on.

Will You Be There?

Will you be there when Jesus calls?
Will your name be on the list?
Is it written down with the saved in Christ?
Are you chosen or will you be missed?

It's time to choose it's time to decide,
Don't let this moment pass.
Make up your mind obey the Lord,
This day might be your last.

Have you read the record of the Lord,
Of His life he willingly gave?
Of the people who rejected him,
The ones he came to save.

It's time to choose it's time to decide,
Don't let this moment pass.
Make up your mind obey the Lord,
This day might be your last.

Will you be like the howling mob,
Hearts hardened and eyes blind?
Or be like the ones who loved the Lord,
And through him, salvation find?

It's time to choose it's time to decide,
Don't let this moment pass.
Make up your mind obey the Lord,
This day might be your last.

Which Path?

Which path will you travel,
Before you reach your goal?
Which path will you travel,
Searching for truth that makes you whole?
Which path will you travel,
To save your eternal soul?
Which path will you travel,
Searching for truth that makes you whole.

The old man sitting wondering
About the value of his life.
Had he done all that was asked him,
Had he alleviated strife?
Was he headed for destruction
In a place where flames do play?
Or was he faithful to the gospel
Which clearly had showed him the way?

Had he stayed faithful to the scriptures,
Or did he fall and snap the chord,
That had joined him to the Father,
And the gift for who endured?
It's a thought that caused him terror
When he remembered what he'd done,
How he'd pursued his earthly riches,
Giving no thought to Gods blest son.

He thought of his decisions,
About how much money he could earn
If he invested all his efforts
To gain all the wealth he'd yearn.
He put first his earthly longings
After all, they filled his need.
Never once a thought of Jesus,
Or the spirits saving seed.

He looked at all his treasure,
At rooms bursting at the seams
With the riches all material,
Not the wealth of the redeemed.
No time for heavenly riches,
And no thought of what's to come.
He ignored the many blessings
Offered by Gods only son.

He's standing at the crossroads,
Deaths finger beckons slow,
His time on earth is ending,
It's time for him to go.
But to where will he be heading,
To which final resting place
Where will his spirit travel,
Hells fire, or Jesus' grace?

He drifts into a coma
Dreams of souls who've left the earth,
Multitudes of drifting spirits,
Crying out for all they're worth.
He feels the heat of fire,
He sees flesh begin to flake.
His blood feels like it's boiling,
How much more can one man take.

The pain it travels through him,
He cries aloud, gnashing his teeth,
He wants to end these feelings,
He starts begging for relief.
Then as quickly as it started,
His vision it did end.
And a place of peace, so tranquil
Into there he did transcend.

A place that's filled with singing,
Angels lifting up their voice,
Giving praise to God almighty,
In his love, they did rejoice.
Nobody there did suffer,
No-one cried aloud with fear,
Each soul was shining brightly
With no need to shed a tear.

Then as he stood there watching,
A voice so gentle he did hear,
He looked around in wonder,
But there was nobody near.
The voice told him to ponder,
About which treasure served him best,
One leading to destruction,
Or one to eternal rest.

At that point he did waken,
His brow shimmering with sweat.
He shouted with excitement,
"I'm alive I'm not dead yet.
I've time to change my future,
God's given me a second chance
I need to change direction,
And my spiritual life enhance.

I cannot love the saviour
And love treasure found on earth,
He's offered wealth untarnished,
He's shown me what I'm worth.
His life for me was given,
He died high on Calvary's hill,
He rose and then ascended
To heaven and loves me still".

Then looking at his treasure,
He knew then that he must share,
With all those who are needy,
And are desperate for care.
His earthly wealth means nothing,
If it costs his spiritual life,
And the sanctuary of heaven,
For an eternity of strife.

We are standing at the crossroads,
Deciding which road, we should take,
The decision it is crucial,
The most important we will make.
Our spirits they are eternal,
Which destination, will we see,
A home of pain and anguish,
Or peace and tranquillity.

A home with all the blessed
Who have all fought the good fight.
And have shone the light of Jesus,
Inside a world of deepest night.
The gospel is Gods' treasure,
To share with listeners far and wide,
And to those who join the faithful,
They'll live with Jesus by their side.

The man did reconsider
His relationship with God,
And his son our saviour Jesus,
Changed the path on which he trod.
He realised the treasure
Offered to us by our Lord,
Is unsurpassed in value
And is found inside his word.

Which path will you travel,
Before you finally reach your goal?
Which path will you travel,
Searching for truth that makes you whole?
Which path will you travel,
To save your eternal soul?
Which path will you travel,
Searching for truth that makes you whole.

Are You Ready?

All that we do one day will cease
We should all make ready,
Those saved in Christ will be at peace,
The ones prepared and ready.
We're given time to get prepared
We can't pretend we have not heard,
No excuse do we have, to be unready.

Those who rejected Jesus' word,
Will regret they were not ready.
They heard the fact that Jesus cared,
Oh, why then, weren't they ready.
They'll find no place on earth to hide,
They'll find themselves all cast outside,
They ignored His word and were not ready.

The clock it ticks, the time soon gone,
Enough time to get ready.
Until He appears, the Blessed One,
To gather who are ready.
Fools say our God does not exist,
They'll find salvation they have missed,
Foolishly they chose, to be unready.

Too late to plead they've had their chance,
Heard warnings to be ready.
Now they can join in Satan's dance,
With all who were not ready.
Eternal dark will smother you,
Jealous now are you of the chosen few?
All those waiting and were ready.

They'll walk the streets of heavenly gold,
Rejoicing they were ready.
No death, no pain, no growing old,
Reward, for being ready.
They'll live with God eternally,
And praise the Holy Trinity,
For steadfastness as they, were making ready.

While reading this it's not too late,
To make plans to be ready.
The Lord is still outside the gate,
Patiently waiting for the ready.
But very soon He will appear,
When the Angels' trumpet you will hear,
Gathering all the saints, those who were ready.

Your action now may be your last,
Are you prepared and ready?
Consider before the die is cast,
Should you be making ready?
One moment here, the next you're gone,
You'll stand before the chosen one,
Will you be prepared; will you be ready?

How Can People Be So Blind?

How can people be so blind?
Why do they choose not to see,
The path that leads the way to life,
The pathway that will set them free?

They walk around ignoring what the scriptures say,
No interest where they'd find the straight and narrow way.
They live to play.

They won't to listen to advice,
They like to wander their own way,
Darkness follows them around,
Living in shadows every day.

They only travel along where the wind does blow,
They do not want to know, their saviour loves them so.
Even though,

He's calls to each one every day,
He wants each person to have heard
How their saviour loves them so
And how much their saviour cared.

He gave his life for all dying on Calvary's tree,
Shed His life-blood so every sinner can be free,
That's you and me.

So, open up your shuttered eyes,
And let the light of Jesus in,
Let him live inside your soul,
Leading you away from sin.

He wants no sinner to perish or to be lost,
His gift is free our Heavenly Father paid the cost,
So, don't be tossed,

Anchor in the sea of life,
To him who steadfastly is sure,
Let him take you by the hand,
To be with Him for evermore.

Don't be so blind don't pretend you cannot see,
Throw off sins chains so you can set you free,
Our saviour died for you and me,
Listen for the saviours loving plea,
Our saviour died for you and me,
Listen for his loving plea.

Where Will You Stand?

Jesus left his home in heaven to show us how to live
He told us of the Fathers love and of how much he had to give.
He walked this earth, showed many signs of his Almighty power
And warned us all to be prepared for judgements awful hour.

Many try and many fail to disprove our Saviours word
They can't accept the glaring fact of just how much he cared.
He went through all the pain and woe and hung upon a cross
To show His love for everyone, so they would not suffer loss.

People close their eyes and ears to Him, ignoring Jesus' call,
They close their minds to the dreadful fact, that they're heading for a fall.
The choice is theirs, the Saviour's tried, he's left it to each one
To choose the path they want to walk before their life's bloods' gone.

But people in their ivory towers corrupt the saviours plan,
Doing their best to divert the path of all of their fellow man.
They preach and tell of other ways that people should be living,
They carry on building up their wealth, while the misguided keep on giving.

Some profess to know much more than he who made each one,
They say the scriptures are only fit for times, that are long gone.
The gospels should forever change, and evolve in modern life,
They take the words that Jesus preached and cut them with a knife.

They prance around in fancy clothes with clowns' hats on their heads,
The rings they wear upon their hands complement their golden threads.
They say they speak the word of God and their lives are oh so pure,
But no one really knows what's going on behind closed doors.

How many have they brainwashed by professing to know all?
How many have they led astray, by perverting Jesus' call?
They say they're special and speak for God, while living on this earth,
And only they can intercede for those of humbler birth.

Those vipers' broods with empty shells, will stand before their God.
Accounting for their deeds on earth, and of the path they trod.
They'll realise when they are there that God had just one plan,
To give salvation, a place in heaven, to every faithful man.

This plan was told as Jesus walked in the lands near Galilee,
Telling how the Father wanted man from sin to be set free.
And to live inside a mansion, He'd prepared in heaven above,
No payment expected from anyone, the mortgage paid with love.

The bible says we shouldn't add to what the scriptures say,
We're told the plan is one that's whole, no part to be thrown away.
The words are there for everyone to read and to decide.
Will you be walking in dead men's shoes, or be there by Jesus side?

The day will come when everyone, will have to give account
Of how they lived while on the earth to God on Zion's mount.
We're told to all who've lived in faith a life of joy He'll give,
Those who chose to ignore His word, will in outer darkness live.

Where will you stand on that awful day when our Christ returns again,
To judge the world and all its deeds, and banish sinful men?
Is it to live within His light, in His heavenly home above?
Or will the outer darkness be your home, outside the Saviours' love?

THANKS

We Thank You Lord Indeed.

For the winter sun that warms us,
Melting snow upon the ground,
For the crops that bring forth harvest,
And birds flying, all around.
For trees and flowers that bloom in springtime,
All grown from a little seed.
For the blessings you pour on us,
We thank you Lord, indeed.

For the planets in the cosmos,
For the stars that shine at night.
For the sun dispelling shadows
Shining majestic, with its light.
For the crops that grow in harvest,
And when from soil they are all freed.
For the blessings you pour on us,
We thank you Lord indeed.

For your promise to your children,
Of your faithful, steadfast love.
And your promise to the faithful,
Of a home in heaven above.
For the sacrifice made for us,
When Christ for us did bleed,
For the blessings you pour on us,
We thank you Lord indeed.

For your help as we all travel,
Along the path of life.
For your spirit who is with us,
And helps when we encounter strife.
For the word which you have left us,
And how for us you intercede.
For the blessings you pour on us,
We thank you Lord indeed.

We Thank You Lord

For morning light that greets our eyes
We thank you Lord,
When a new born baby cries,
We thank you Lord,
For the blessings sent each day
As you guide us on our way,
For your faithfulness and love
We thank you Lord.

We thank you Lord your blessings are free,
We thank you Lord Christ died on that tree.
We thank you Lord He rose again,
We thank you Lord, in heaven He'll reign.
We thank you Lord sins you'll forgive,
We thank you Lord for the love you give.

For all the food we eat,
We thank you Lord,
For the shoes upon our feet,
We thank you Lord.
For your son who for us died,
After His birching, crucified,
For Him raising back to life
We thank you Lord.

We thank you Lord your blessings are free,
We thank you Lord Christ died on that tree.
We thank you Lord He rose again,
We thank you Lord, in heaven He'll reign.
We thank you Lord sins you'll forgive,
We thank you Lord for the love you give.

For your promise to forgive,
We thank you Lord,
For your lessons on how to live,
We thank you Lord.
For your steadfast faithful love,
Promise of a home with you above,
For your purity and grace,
We thank you Lord.

We thank you Lord your blessings are free,
We thank you Lord Christ died on that tree.
We thank you Lord He rose again,
We thank you Lord, in heaven He'll reign.
We thank you Lord sins you'll forgive,
We thank you Lord for the love you give.

We Will Sing the Songs of Angels

One day as I was walking,
Through my lonely life of shame,
I heard a voice which told me,
Jesus Christ will come again.

I then stopped what I was doing,
Listened eagerly to the words,
Saying God is standing waiting,
For those who Jesus' blood has spared.

We will sing the songs of angels,
As we sit beneath his throne,
Praising God, the one who saved us,
And has welcomed each one home.

His body it was beaten,
But throughout our saviour cared,
He knew that He should finish
The promise in God's word.

He will return in glory,
Claiming those who are His own,
And they'll gather with the Angels,
Singing praises round His throne.

We will sing the songs of angels,
As we sit beneath his throne,
Praising God, the one who saved us,
And has welcomed each one home.

We will walk with him in heaven,
Along the shining streets of gold,
We will see its wondrous beauty,
And it's glory we'll behold.

Everything the Lord has promised,
Will one day be revealed,
The saved will be in heaven,
And by His love be sealed.

We will sing the songs of angels,
As we sit beneath His throne,
Praising God, the one who saved us,
And has welcomed each one home.

He Is My Saviour.

He is my saviour, my blessed saviour,
He walks beside me and guides my way.
He proved just how much, he really loved me,
When he gave his life for me that day
Each day I pass through
Life's earthly shadows,
And sins temptations
They slow me down.
I never fear,
For, He's there to guide me,
Along the pathway that leads to my crown.

He is my saviour, my blessed saviour,
He walks beside me and guides my way.
He proved just how much, he really loved me,
When he gave his life for me that day
There is nobody
I can rely on
Who is more faithful
Than Christ my Lord,
And He has promised,
To all the faithful,
They'll receive in heaven their blessed reward.

He is my saviour, my blessed saviour,
He walks beside me and guides my way.
He proved just how much, he really loved me,
When he gave his life for me that day.
As days go by, my
Love it gets stronger
As He gives blessings
To me each day
If I need help I
Know He will listen
When I fall on my knees and I pray.

He is my saviour, my blessed saviour,
He walks beside me and guides my way.
He proved just how much, He really loved me,
When He gave His life for me that day.
He's given to us,
A book of scripture,
To guide us all as
We walk along,
If we are faithful
To what is written,
One day we'll all sing the heavenly song.

He is my saviour, my blessed saviour,
He walks beside me and guides my way.
He proved just how much, he really loved me,
When he gave his life for me that day.

EPILOGUE

May You

May your day be filled with laughter,
And your hours be filled with love.
May you be bathed in heavenly blessings,
Sent by your Father, from above.
May your strong steps never falter,
On the straight and narrow path before
You reach your destination,
Found behind heavens golden door.
May you stand before the Father,
When you've finished your holy race,
May you wonder in his glory,
When you see your saviours' face.
May his radiant smile be on you,
As he gives the crown of life,
To you who's remained faithful,
Throughout all your earthly life.

May

May the peace of the Lord be always with you,
May its joy inspire and uplift your soul,
May its steadfastness guide and protect you,
May the spirit of God keep you whole.

May His light shine and guide you through the darkness,
May His hand steady you, and keep you calm,
May His spirit keep you safe from danger,
May His protection keep your soul from harm.

May His love be your friend all your journey,
May He guide all your steps to heaven's door,
May the voice of the saviour bid "welcome",
May you reside with the saints evermore.

May you observe Jesus there basked in His glory,
May you join in with the throng 'round His throne.
May you sing songs of blest adoration,
May He welcome you to your heavenly home.

God Is.

God is our father,
He encourages and supports us growing up in His faith.
He supplies our every daily need.
He knows each unspoken heart's desire.
God is there to help us; he's there to light our way,
He's all we can rely on; he'll always answer when we pray.

God is our refuge,
He is our shield against the arrows of the wicked one.
He is our anchor in the seas of life,
He offers to us shelter, as life's storm winds daily blow.
God is there to help us; he's there to light our way,
He's all we can rely on; he'll always answer when we pray.

God is our protection
He guards us against those who follow the evil one,
He protects as we daily preach His word.
He strengthens when fatigue rents and tears our spirit.
God is there to help us; he's there to light our way,
He's all we can rely on; he'll always answer when we pray.

God is our life's guide.
He leads us as we walk His way, keeping to the narrow path.
He keeps us all from stumbling.
He offers His hand to keep us safe.
God is there to help us; he's there to light our way,
He's all we can rely on; he'll always answer when we pray.

God is our truth.
He promised men in olden days, he'd provide what they did need.
He gave them all they asked in his name.
He keeps his word always.
God is there to help us; he's there to light our way,
He's all we can rely on; he'll always answer when we pray.

God is our light.
He lights our way as we take steps in this dark and sinful world.
He helps us to break down Satan's walls.
He illuminates our path.
God is there to help us; he's there to light our way,
Hc's all we can rely on; he'll always answer when we pray.

God is our salvation.
He sent his son to be the saviour of this sin sodden world.
He watched as He died on the cross.
He raised Him from the dead.
God is there to help us; he's there to light our way,
He's all we can rely on; he'll always answer when we pray.

God is our hope.
He showed by sending us His son, He has unconditional love.
He has loved us from the very start.
He is our only hope.
God is there to help us; he is there to light our way,
He is all we can rely on; he'll always answer when we pray.

Lead Us Home

Oh, blessed Lord, we cannot live without thee,
Our hearts will beat each day, like empty drums,
We'll have no hope, if you're not there beside us,
Please never leave, we're lost when on our own.

Please take control, and guide us through the darkness,
Let your light shine, illuminate our path.
For we'd be lost if you're not there beside us,
Please lead us home, dear saviour lead us home.

Like leaves from trees, we fall with no direction,
We're blown around where're the wind does blow.
We have no home, no lasting firm foundation,
Without you Lord, we have no heavenly home.

Please take control, help us be sure and steadfast,
Give us your strength to fight the evil foe,
Help us resist temptations that are scattered,
Along the pathway, to our heavenly home.

Please take control and lead us through the darkness,
Let your light shine, illuminate our path.
Lord take control help us be sure and steadfast,
And lead us onward, to our heavenly home.

And lead us onward to our heavenly home.

Salvation

Search for the truth that sets you free,
Allow your chains to be released.
Let your inner being accept the truth,
Verifying each lesson you've learnt.
Always look towards heaven,
Have strength temptations to repel.
I was the person you were
Open yourself to become a new you,
Now is the time to decide.

Printed in Poland
by Amazon Fulfillment
Poland Sp. z o.o., Wrocław